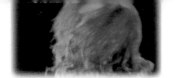

tori amos

collectibles

by Paul Campbell

TORI AMOS:
Collectibles

by
Paul Campbell

Order No. OP 47869
US ISBN: 0.8256.1578.X
UK ISBN: 0.7119.6174.3

Exclusive Distributors:
Music Sales Corporation
257 Park Avenue South,
New York, NY 10010 USA
Book Sales Limited
8/9 Frith Street, London W1V 5TZ England
Music Sales Pty. Limited
120 Rothschild Street, Rosebery,
Sydney, NSW 2018, Australia

Color separations by Color 4 Graphics
Printed in the United States of America by
Vicks Lithograph and Printing Corporation

To contact the author, you can e-mail him at:
toriinfo@worldnet.att.net

acknowledgements

A very special thanks to Tom Richards at Upside Down in the US and Robin Evans at Take To The Sky in the UK. Without Tom and Robin's help and guidance—this book would not have been possible.

Thanks to Rob Kistner, Dan Earley and John Young for making it all come together.

Thanks to Barrie Edwards, Kalen Rogers, Todd Marconi, Greg Hoogheem, Vince De Leon, Jim Manfre, Roseann Salvagno, Ken Schoenwetter, Kathy Warner, Liz Russell, Scott Wolf, Melanie Ince, Charles Donohoe, Neale Parker, Marian Cross, Rick Sudakoff, Hari Kousaros, Dave Levesque, Wayne Rubenstein, Atlantic Records, East West Records and especially thanks to Tori for giving us so much to work with and all her years.

introduction

"Making love to the piano…one of my more attractive minor accomplishments" [†]

Tori Amos exploded out of anonymity early in 1992 into seemingly overnight commercial success. After resurrecting and reinventing herself from the relative obscurity and instant cut-out status of *Y Kant Tori Read*, Tori released *Little Earthquakes* to an unsuspecting world. Instantly she was everywhere, playing live to thousands of new fans all over the planet in an apparently endless tour that would have broken a less resilient performer. The press loved her but for the most part, labeled her weird. Tori's fans didn't try to label her, they just loved her. Contrary to many record executives' ways of thinking, the "girl and her piano thing" had indeed happened.

Tori has been extraordinarily generous in the quality and quantity of work she has given her fans. In her relatively short major-label career, Tori has recorded and released an amazing amount of material. To be a Tori Amos completist is a very expensive, involved and never-ending pursuit. The extensive number of unreleased B sides and live tracks alone dwarf the entire works of many other "major" artists. Tori has always taken her fans' interests extremely close to heart. She has spent so much time on the road—performing for countless numbers of people—that it is no small wonder she enjoys the remarkable adulation given her throughout the world.

There has been much written about Tori Amos, the artist and musician, in the last few years but not a great quantity of collective detail regarding the actual product Tori has recorded and released. This book is the what, where and when of the works of Tori Amos. We have made every effort for the information contained herein to be as accurate and as complete as possible. Any additional information will be welcomed and can be sent to us at toriinfo@worldnet.att.net.

I have purposely left out setting a value on the items contained in this guide. I feel that it is irrelevant for two reasons. One, the price an item is worth in 1997 is not what it will be worth in 2001 or even 1998. Secondly, value means nothing compared to availability. In 1994, the *Baltimore* 7" single was valued at £100 in a UK magazine. There a lot of Tori fans who have £100 in hand, ready to buy, but there aren't any *Baltimore* 7" singles for sale, are there? For these reasons I feel setting a price on the items in this book would be confusing at best.

Two of the best sources for obtaining Tori CDs, vinyl and promotional items are *Record Collector* magazine in the UK and *Goldmine* magazine in the US.

Paul Campbell — December, 1996

[†] *Van Heflin treating Joan Crawford to Schumann in the 1947 film "Possessed."*

contents

one 1

chapter one
the albums

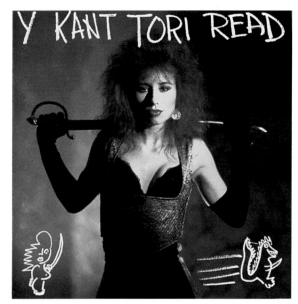

US CD (Front)

US CD (Back)

US CD (Disc)

Y Kant Tori Read

(*US*) Atlantic:
81845-1 (LP)
81845-2 (CD)
81845-4 (CS)

Atlantic Records released *Y Kant Tori Read* in July 1988. The album was preceded by the single *The Big Picture* released one month earlier in June. *Y Kant Tori Read* was released in all three formats, LP, CD and cassette. The name *Y Kant Tori Read* was Tori's ambiguous reference to her days at The Peabody Conservatory when she refused to read music; although she was thoroughly capable of doing so. The band consisted of studio musicians thrown together by producer Joe Chiccarelli, who had previously produced Pat Benatar. Tori sang, played piano and wrote all the tracks except for co-writing four tracks with ex-Poco member Kim Bullard and one track with Brad Cobb. The album was produced and recorded by Joe Chiccarelli at Hollywood Sound Studio in Los Angeles. At this point in her career Tori was not yet calling the shots and worked with whomever Atlantic Records saw fit to throw into the mix. The band included Steve Caton, who would continue to work with Tori on the next three albums and in fact play guitar on the *Boys for Pele* tour in 1996. Also included were Matt Sorum (who would go on to play drums in Guns & Roses and The Cult), Steve Farris (Mr. Mister) and Kim Bullard.

Putting aside the severe metal-babe image projected on the cover and the seriously pouting vixen on the back of the album, *Y Kant Tori Read* actually contained a few non-lethal tracks. *The Etienne Trilogy* would not be too far out of place on *Little Earthquakes*, and *The Big Picture* as well as *Cool On Your Island* have a certain edge to them (although it helps to listen to *The Big Picture* if you are watching the video at the same time). Unfortunately, the rest of the album is a tough listen at best. Most copies of the LP that are found today are promotional copies because the album sold poorly. Because of this, commercial (non-promotional) copies of *Y Kant Tori Read* are scarce. There were 3800 CDs, 3300 LPs and 3200 cassettes pressed. The cassettes are even harder to find than the LP, and again promotional cassettes appear more frequently than commercial copies. The CD is practically non-existent and commands a price that has climbed into the hundreds of dollars. The CD has been bootlegged in several different versions (See Chapter 8). Finding an original Atlantic CD sealed in a long box is virtually impossible.

Tori has been asked frequently about the re-release of *Y Kant Tori Read* and has stated that "It's not going to happen." The only possibility for an official Atlantic re-issue might be if Tori were to change labels at some point in the future and Atlantic would miraculously resurrect this "lost" album. However, that situation seems highly unlikely at best.

US LP (Front)

US LP (Back)

US LP (Left Side [A])

US LP (Right Side [B])

Track Listing (*CD tracks in parentheses.*)

Left Side (A)
1 The Big Picture (4:19)
Tori Amos & Kim Bullard
2 Cool on Your Island (4:57)
Tori Amos & Kim Bullard
3 Fayth (4:23)
Tori Amos & Brad Cobb
4 Fire on the Side (4:53)
Tori Amos
5 Pirates (4:16)
Tori Amos & Kim Bullard

Right Side (B)
1(6) Floating City (5:22)
Tori Amos
2(7) Heart Attack at 23 (5:16)
Tori Amos
3(8) On The Boundary (4:38)
Tori Amos
4(9) You Go To My Head (3:55)
Tori Amos
5(10) Etienne Trilogy (6:45)
    The Highlands
    Tori Amos & Kim Bullard
    Etienne
    Skyboat Song
    Traditional

US CD Long Box (Front)

US CD Long Box (Back)

US Cassette

3

Little Earthquakes

(*US*) Atlantic: 82358-2 (CD), 82358-4 (CS), 82358-8 (MD)
Record Club: BMG D150382 (CD)
(*Canada*) CD82358 (CD)
(*UK*) East West: 82358-1 (LP), 82358-2 (CD), 82358-4 (CS)
(*Japan*) East West: WMC5-488 (CD)

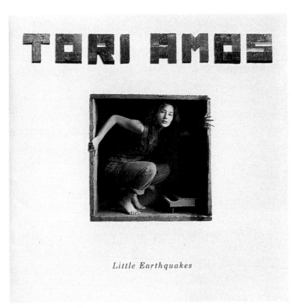

Little Earthquakes

US CD (Front)

US CD (Disc)

In late 1990 Tori came back to Atlantic Records with a 10-track demo tape, several years in the making, that would later become the essence of *Little Earthquakes* and its subsequent B sides. The track listing consisted of *Russia* (later to become *Take To The Sky*) / *Mary* / *Crucify* / *Happy Phantom* / *Leather* / *Winter* / *Sweet Dreams* / *Song For Eric* / *Learn To Fly* / *Flying Dutchman*.

After the commercial failure of *Y Kant Tori Read*, Tori had taken some time off to re-invent herself and in the process, dropped the band and got back in touch with her genuine passion, the piano. Many of these songs are different from the released versions. Some are longer, some are mixed differently, many have different lyrics. *Winter*, for example, has percussion and tambourine accompanying it throughout. *Flying Dutchman* is warmer and the vocals are far more pronounced than the later version. *Learn To Fly* has still to see a release anywhere.

Atlantic Records' Doug Morris, still unhappy because he wanted a female Elton John, decided at this point that Tori might be a little too eccentric for America. Morris shipped Tori off to London, where being eccentric is the rule rather than the exception. As a result of this move Tori was able to work and perform in an atmosphere much more to her liking than the insincerity of Los Angeles.

Tori next played a private, candlelit show for East West Records' managing director Max Hole. Hole needed no more

convincing that East West had someone very special in their midst. East West, Atlantic's UK partner, insisted that Tori begin playing live in and around London to accrue media attention for her. Playing even small clubs in London usually brings someone from the music press. The raves quickly began to accumulate for Tori. At one point Tori actually invited several music journalists to her flat for private concerts and tea. Once the UK press fell in love with her, the girl was off and running.

Little Earthquakes was released in the UK on January 13th 1992 and in the US in early February. The album was preceded by two singles, *Me And A Gun* in October 1991 and *Silent All These Years* in November. The wonderous *Little Earthquakes* only reached number 54 in the US but climbed to number 14 in the UK charts. The British, always ready to embrace something new and strange, had taken to Tori like mad. Hence, Atlantic's gamble of moving Tori to London had paid off very well.

It didn't take long, though, before word of mouth, alternative radio and a short 17-city promotional tour of America had everyone buzzing about this angst-ridden singer who wore her album on her sleeve. Tori had her foot in the door and would never look back. *Little Earthquakes* produced a treasure trove of singles and the accompanying unreleased tracks, cover versions, remixes and live cuts.

Little Earthquakes was entirely written by Tori and produced in part

US Mini Disc (Front)

US Mini-Disc (Back)

US CD (First Pressing)

by Tori, Davitt Sigerson, Eric Rosse and Ian Stanley with noted UK producer Jon Kelly mixing *Girl* and *Winter*. Worth noting: initial commercial pressings of the CD in the US were accidentally shipped as promotional copies. The difference between these and later pressings is the line "1992 ATLANTIC RECORDING CORPORATION • FOR PROMOTIONAL USE ONLY • NOT FOR SALE • PRINTED IN USA ON RECYCLED PAPER" printed in very small print in the lower-left-hand corner of the CD insert. In addition, all the photos in that insert are in black and white; later inserts are in color. In the US, only CD, cassette and later, Mini-Disc were released but in Europe an LP was issued. The lyrics and photos from the insert are printed on the back of the album cover instead of the phallic plant-like object that graces the back of the CD. The German version of the *Little Earthquakes* LP was actually released on the Atlantic label. All other European releases were through East/West, making the German variation unique.

The *Little Earthquakes* Mini-Disc wasn't released until 1993 in the US. In theory a great idea, Mini-Discs have not quite caught on and are unlikely to be around for long since the hardware remains expensive, the selection of titles is very limited and the feeling is that we really don't need another format.

Little Earthquakes reached platinum record status in the US, (over 1 million copies) and has sold over 2 million copies worldwide.

US Mini-Disc (Disc Front)

US Mini Disc (Disc Back)

Track Listing:

Side One
1. Crucify (4:58)
2. Girl (4:06)
3. Silent All These Years (4:11)
4. Precious Things (4:26)
5. Winter (5:41)
6. Happy Phantom (3:13)

Side Two
1(7) China (4:59)
2(8) Leather (3:12)
3(9) Mother (6:59)
4(10) Tear In Your Hand (4:38)
5(11) Me And A Gun (3:44)
6(12) Little Earthquakes (6:51)

Japanese CD (Front and Spine)

Brazilian LP (Back)

Japanese CD (Disc)

UK LP (Front)

UK LP (Back)

UK LP (Side 1)

UK LP (Side 2)

Canadian CD (Disc)

UK Cassette (Front)

UK Cassette (Back)

US Cassette

German Atlantic LP (A-Side)

German Atlantic LP (B-Side)

US CD Long Box

German CD (Disc)

Under The Pink

(*US*) Atlantic: 82567-1 (LP), 82567-2 (CD), 82567-4 (CS)
Record Club: BMG D102480 (CD)
(*Canada*) East West: CD82567 (CD)
(*UK*) East West: 82567-1 (LP), 82567-2 (CD), 82567-4 (CS)
(*Japan*) East West: AMCE-653 (CD)

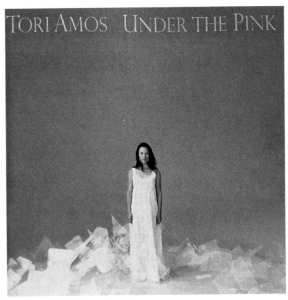

US CD (Front)

Under The Pink was released first in the UK on January 31st 1994, February 1st in the US and finally in Japan on February 25th. This time, propelled by the early January release of the anxiously awaited new single *Cornflake Girl*, Tori went straight to number one in the UK. In the US, *Under The Pink* only reached number 12 as a result of less enthusiastic radio play for the first US single *God*, released in February. The extraordinary *Under The Pink* was quite a different album from its predecessor. While getting mixed reviews from the press this time around, it still managed to go platinum and sell over 1.2 million copies in the US and over 2 million worldwide.

The album was finally titled *Under The Pink*, after another title—'*God With A Big G*'—was contemplated and rejected. *Under The Pink* was entirely written by Tori and produced by Tori and Eric Rosse. Trent Reznor also appears, contributing background vocals on *Past The Mission*. The album was recorded in New Mexico and Los Angeles; strings were added in Los Angeles and mixed in London.

The original cover for *Under The Pink* was scrapped because Tori thought the cover photo of her was a little too alluring, which was not the message she was trying to get across with the album. A very small number of pre-release cassettes with this cover made it out, but virtually all the CDs were destroyed. Pre-release CDs therefore were shipped with no insert in a jewel box, just a white CD with Tori's name, the title and track listing. *Under The Pink*

yielded an impressive array of singles with still more unreleased tracks, cover versions, live material and some elaborate packaging contained in coveted limited edition singles from the UK.

Supporting *Under The Pink*, Tori embarked on a 11-month 170-date tour that saw her cross the US twice as well as playing to audiences in Canada, Europe, Japan, Australia and New Zealand. It was an exhausting schedule, sometimes encompassing two shows a night, that helped earn her legions of new fans as well as pushing sales of *Under The Pink* past platinum. Initially only released on CD and cassette in the US, Atlantic saw an opportunity to fill in the gap between albums and take advantage of the resurgent popularity of vinyl by releasing a limited edition (25,000) pink vinyl pressing of *Under The Pink* in late summer 1995. The album itself is a brilliant pink color with a red Atlantic label. The artwork is essentially the same as the UK vinyl released 18 months earlier.

US CD (Disc)

US LP and Cover

UK LP (Front)

UK LP (Back)

UK LP (A-Side)

UK LP (B-Side)

US Pink Vinyl LP (Side 1)

US Pink Vinyl LP (Side 2)

Japanese CD (Front and Spine)

Track Listing

Side One
1. Pretty Good Year (3:25)
2. God (3:58)
3. Bells For Her (5:20)
4. Past The Mission (4:05)
5. Baker Baker (3:20)
6. The Wrong Band (3:03)
7. The Waitress (3:09)

Side Two
1(8) Cornflake Girl (5:06)
2(9) Icicle (5:47)
3(10) Cloud On My Tongue (4:44)
4(11) Space Dog (5:10)
5(12) Yes, Anastasia (9:33)

Canadian CD (Disc)

US Cassette

French Cassette

9

Under The Pink and More Pink

(*Australia*) East West: 756780607-2 (2-CD)

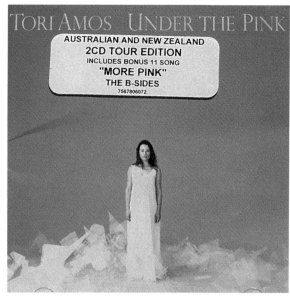

Under The Pink And More Pink CD (Front)

Under The Pink And More Pink CD
(Disc 1)

Under The Pink And More Pink CD
(Disc 2)

East West Australia produced a limited 2-CD tour edition called *Under The Pink and More Pink* to coincide with Tori's 1994 Australasian tour. This unique package included an excellent 11-track bonus disc of B sides including the previously commercially unavailable *Little Drummer Boy*. The discs were housed in a thin double jewel case with the 1994 Australian and New Zealand tour dates on the inside back cover. The bonus disc was called *More Pink: "The B-Sides."* This compilation was compiled specifically for this release.

Track Listing

CD 1: Under The Pink
1 Pretty Good Year (3:25)
2 God (3:58)
3 Bells For Her (5:20)
4 Past The Mission (4:05)
5 Baker Baker (3:20)
6 The Wrong Band (3:03)
7 The Waitress (3:09)
8 Cornflake Girl (5:06)
9 Icicle (5:47)
10 Cloud On My Tongue (4:44)
11 Space Dog (5:10)
12 Yes, Anastasia (9:33)

CD 2: More Pink: "The B-Sides"
1 A Case Of You (4:38)
2 Honey (3:47)
3 Daisy Dead Petals (3:02)
4 Sister Janet (4:02)
5 Sugar (4:27)
6 Take To The Sky (4:20)
7 Upside Down (4:22)
8 Flying Dutchman (6:31)
9 Here. in my Head (Live 6:05)
10 Black Swan (4:04)
11 Little Drummer Boy (3:20)

Under The Pink & Little Earthquakes

(*Australia*) East West: 756780633-2 (2-CD)
Reissue (*Australia*) East West: 756780681-2 (2-CD)

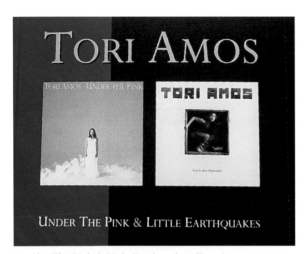

Under The Pink & Little Earthquakes (Front)

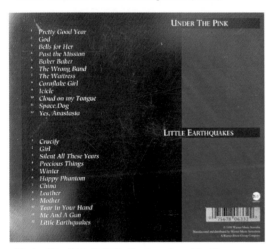

Under The Pink & Little Earthquakes (Back)

Under The Pink & Little Earthquakes was released as a double CD in Australia as part of a Warner-Elektra-Atlantic budget series nicely packaged in a double jewel case. The package includes the complete lyric books from both albums and retains the album's original track listings. Originally released in 1995 and then reissued in late 1996 as *Little Earthquakes & Under The Pink* with a different cover, new catalog number and the title, reversed from the previous version.

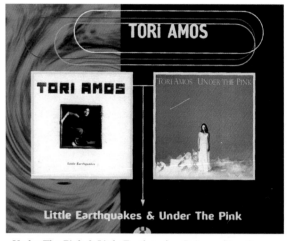

Under The Pink & Little Earthquakes Reissue (Front)

Under The Pink & Little Earthquakes CD
(Disc 1)

Under The Pink & Little Earthquakes CD
(Disc 2)

Boys For Pele

(*US*) Atlantic 82862-1 (LP), 82862-2 (CD), 82862-4 (CS)
Record Club: Columbia House: 147090 (CD)
(*UK*) East West: 82862-1 (LP), 82862-2 (CD), 82862-4 (CS)
(*Japan*) AMCE-918 (CD)

US CD (Front)

US CD (Disc)

Boys For Pele was released on January 22nd in the UK, January 23rd in the US and February 25th in Japan. The album made it to number one in the UK and reached number two in the US. *Boys For Pele* sold an impressive 110,000 copies in its first week of release and had sold more than 1 million copies by June. The first single, *Caught A Lite Sneeze*, preceded the album by three weeks. *Caught a Lite Sneeze* was released in January both in the US, and as a two-part UK single. This time Atlantic treated vinyl junkies to a beautiful limited edition double album in the UK and US. The records themselves are a beautiful clear pale-green vinyl in the US and clear vinyl in the UK. The album also contains an insert, with the lyrics on one side and on the reverse, a photo of Tori that also appears on the inside back cover of the CD insert. There were stamped promotional copies of the vinyl distributed, although the promos are the same as commercial copies except for the promotional stamp.

For the first time, the Japanese[†] version of a Tori Amos CD contained a bonus track; *Toodles Mr.*

US Cassette

Jim, one of the B sides of the UK *Caught A Lite Sneeze* CD single, was added as the extra track.

The LPs varied from the CD in that the tracks marked with [†] were not given numbers. Tori intended to open each side of the vinyl with a short introduction track to the rest of the songs on each side, although *Beauty Queen* segues into *Horses* with no break. The final track, *Twinkle*, is also not given a track number on vinyl. Only one song on the CD, *Beauty Queen*, is not given a track number.

All the *Boys For Pele* album tracks were written by Tori, and for the first time, Tori produced the album herself. Another addition to this album was Tori's use of some new keyboard variaties: a harpsichord on *Blood Roses*, *Professional Widow*, *Caught A Lite Sneeze* and *In The Springtime Of His Voodoo*; a Harmonium organ on *Hey Jupiter*, *Blood Roses*, *Muhammad My Friend*; and a clavichord on *Little Amsterdam*.

Boys For Pele included church bells, horns, strings, a gospel choir and bagpipes. Steve Caton handled the guitars and would join Tori on the road for the *Boys For Pele* tour. Principal recording was done in a church in County Wicklow, Ireland, a rented house in County Cork, Ireland, with the remainder in New Orleans, LA USA. Future pressings of *Boys For Pele* will replace the original version of *Talula* with *Talula* (*The Tornado Mix* 3:43).

UK CD with Talula Remix (Back)

Track Listing:

Side A
 Beauty Queen
1 Horses (6:07)
2 Blood Roses (3:56)
3 Father Lucifer (3:43)
4 Professional Widow (4:31)

Side B
‡(5) Mr. Zebra (1:07)
1(6) Marianne (4:07)
2(7) Caught A Lite Sneeze (4:24)
3(8) Muhammad My Friend (3:48)
4(9) Hey Jupiter (5:10)

Side C
‡(10) Way Down (1:13)
1(11) Little Amsterdam (4:29)
2(12) Talula (4:08)
3(13) Not The Red Baron (3:49)

Side D
‡(14) Agent Orange (1:26)
1(15) Doughnut Song (4:19)
2(16) In The Springtime Of His Voodoo (5:32)
3(17) Putting The Damage On (5:08
‡(18) Twinkle (3:12)
(19) Toodles Mr. Jim (3:09) (*Japanese CD only*)

† *The Japanese often add a bonus track(s) to their CDs to make them more desirable in Japan than the cheaper imports that find their way into the country from the US and elsewhere. The Japanese versions of* Little Earthquakes *and* Under the Pink, *however, contained no bonus tracks. The paper sash that covers one end of the CD is called an obi, Japanese for "belt." These are provided to display the CDs in Japanese shops according to the Japanese spelling of the artist's name.*

Japanese CD (Back)

UK CD with Talula Remix (Disc)

Japanese CD (Disc)

Japanese CD (Front and Spine)

US 2-LP (Front)   US 2-LP (Back)

US Clear Green Vinyl (US Cover and LP)   US Clear Green Vinyl (Side A)

UK Clear Vinyl (UK Cover and LP)   UK Clear Vinyl LP (Side A)

chapter two
singles and ep's

Ellen Amos

Baltimore (US)

7" Single
MEA Records
MEA5290
Released 1980

    1 Baltimore (3:31)
    2 Walking With You (4:28)

Baltimore, still the rarest and most unobtainable Tori single, because there are fewer than ten in circulation, was written in 1980 in response to a Baltimore city contest to come up with a theme song for the city and is quite different from anything Tori has recorded since. The B side, *Walking With You*, is a much more middle-of-the-road love song. It's quite pleasant, clearly showing promise of what's to come. Financed by her father, *Baltimore* was pressed on their new 'MEA' (for Myra Ellen Amos) label.

US 7" A-Side

US 7" B-Side

Y Kant Tori Read

The Big Picture (US)

7" Single
Atlantic 7-89086
June 1988

    1 The Big Picture (4:19)
    2 You Go To My Head (3:55)

Tori's first major label single. Atlantic didn't think it warranted a picture sleeve, although the promotional-only 12" did have one. Atlantic also shot a promotional video in May to accompany the single. *The Big Picture*, Tori's first video, was directed by Marty Callner, who would later find success directing Aerosmith's videos.

US 7" A-Side

US 7" B-Side

Cool On Your Island (US)

7" Single
Atlantic 7-89021
August 1988

    1 Cool On Your Island (4:57)
    2 Heart Attack At 23 (5:16)

Tori's second single and first commercial picture sleeve. Like its predecessor, the single went nowhere—this time no video was shot. Atlantic had pretty much given up at this point after working the *Y Kant Tori Read* album a mere two months.

US 7" Sleeve (Front)

US 7" A-Side

US 7" Sleeve (Back)

US 7" B-Side

Little Earthquakes

Me And A Gun (UK)

CD Single
East West YZ618CD
October 1991

12" Single
East West YZ618T

    1 Silent All These Years (4:11)
    2 Upside Down (4:22)
    3 Me And A Gun (3:42)
    4 Thoughts (2:36)

7" Single
East West YZ618

    1 Silent All These Years (4:11)
    2 Me and A Gun (3:42)

Me And A Gun, the hopelessly unlikely choice for a debut single, was released in the UK on October 21st 1991. Tori's name did not appear on the front of the single, only the title, *Me And A Gun*. One of the B sides, *Silent All These Years*, was added at Radio One in the UK and there named "Record Of The Week." This single would be re-issued the following month renamed *Silent All These Years* with Tori's name added to the cover and a cassette single added. A title sticker was added to the 7" single reading "Tori Amos *Silent All These Years*" because that was the track that radio had picked up on. People were having trouble finding the single in stores, hence the sticker. The beautiful *Upside Down* would go on to become many fans' favorite B side. Indeed, it is the only track Tori later regretted leaving off the album. *Thoughts* is another non-LP track. The 12" single of *Me And A Gun* is particularly scarce.

UK CD Single (Front)

UK CD Single (Back)

UK CD Single (Disc)

UK 12" Single (Front)

UK 12" Single (Back)

UK 12" Single (A-Side)

UK 7" Single (Front)

UK 12" Single (B-Side)

Me And A Gun (Germany)

CD Single
East West 75559-2
October 1991

1 Silent All These Years (4:13)
2 Upside Down (4:22)
3 Me And A Gun (3:42)
4 Thoughts (2:36)

The German *Me And A Gun* contains the same tracks as the UK version, the only differences being the UK catalog numbers and that the CD is not a picture CD.

German CD Single (Front and Spine)

German CD Single (Back)

German CD Single (Disc)

Silent All These Years (UK)

CD Single
East West YZ618CD
November 1991
(*Re-issue of* Me And A Gun)

12" Single
East West YZ618T

1 Silent All These Years (4:11)
2 Upside Down (4:22)
3 Me And A Gun (3:42)
4 Thoughts (2:36)

7" Single
East West YZ618

Cassette Single
East West YZ618C

1 Silent All These Years (4:11)
2 Me and A Gun (3:42)

This, the first UK release of *Silent All These Years* is the same single as *Me And A Gun* except the packaging has been altered to rename it *Silent All These Years* and to add Tori's name to the cover. The disc itself is identical to *Me And A Gun*, a picture disc of a lock of brilliant orange hair surrounding the disc. The insert contains the lyrics to *Silent All These Years*. The re-issue of *Silent All These Years* the following August would not contain lyrics or a picture CD although the track listing would remain unchanged.

UK CD Single First Pressing (Front)

Silent All These Years (Australia)

Cassette Single
East West 76014-4
December 1991

1 Silent All These Years (4:11)
2 Me And A Gun (3:42)

Tori's first Australian single was only released on cassette and duplicated the UK cassette and 7" single tracks.

UK 12" (Front)

UK 12" (Back)

UK CD Single First Pressing (Disc)

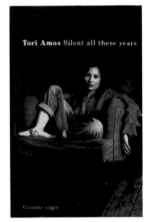

Australian Cassette Single
(Front)

UK 7" First Pressing (Front)

Australian Cassette Single
(Back)

UK 7" First Pressing (Back)

China(UK)

CD Single
East West A7531CD
January 1992

12" Single
East West A7531T

    1 China (5:01)
    2 Sugar (4:27)
    3 Flying Dutchman (6:31)
    4 Humpty Dumpty (2:52)

7" Single
East West A7531

Cassette Single
East West A7531C

    1 China (5:01)
    2 Sugar (4:27)

Tori's third UK single, the exquisite *China*, sadly only reached number 51 in the UK charts. The single included the magnificent and previously unreleased B sides *Sugar* and *Flying Dutchman* as well as Tori's curious interpretation of *Humpty Dumpty*. The UK *China* CD single is packaged in a jewel box. *China* would be the last 12" single released until *God* in August 1994.

UK CD Single (Front)

UK CD Single (Disc)

UK CD Single (Back)

UK 7" Single (Front)

UK 7" Single (A-Side)

UK Cassette Single

UK 7" Single (Back)

UK 7" Single (B-Side)

UK 12" Single (Front)

UK 12" Single (Back)

UK 12" Single (A-Side)

UK 12" Single (B-Side)

China (Germany)

CD Single
East West 85905
January 1992

1 China (5:01)
2 Sugar (4:27)
3 Flying Dutchman (6:31)
4 Humpty Dumpty (2:52)

The German version of the *China* CD single comes packaged in a slim jewel-case. The track listing remained the same as the UK version.

German CD Single (Front)

German CD Single (Back)

German CD Single (First Press Disc)

German CD Single (Second Press Disc)

China (France)

CD Single
East West/Carrere 85755-2
January 1992

Cassette Single
East West/Carrere 85755-4

1 China (Edit 3:55)
2 Flying Dutchman (Edit 6:29)

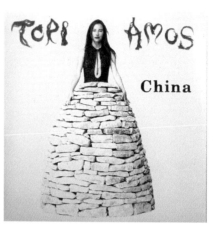

French CD Single (Front)

The French *China* CD single comes in a cardboard sleeve featuring an edited (3:55) version of *China* and according to the sleeve, an edited (6:29) version of *Flying Dutchman*. The actual timing of *Flying Dutchman* is 6:31, so the sleeve is a misprint[†]. *Flying Dutchman*, being a B side was never issued in an edited version. The graphics on the French version are unique, in that they place Tori's name at the top of the sleeve instead of the bottom as on all other releases. The title, *China*, appears on the right-hand side of the sleeve as opposed to the left side on previous releases. The lettering is far bolder and more prominent than the UK or German versions. The cassette single was packaged in a blister pack. The French *Crucify* and *Cornflake Girl* cassette singles were also packaged this way.

[†] *Timings frequently vary incorrectly when the same single is issued in several countries.*

French CD Single (Back)

French CD Single (Disc)

French Cassette Single

Winter (UK)

CD Single Part 1
East West A7504CD
March 1992

> 1 Winter (5:44)
> 2 The Pool (2:51)
> 3 Take To The Sky (4:20)
> 4 Sweet Dreams (3:27)

CD Single Part 2 (Limited Edition)
East West A7504CDX

> 1 Winter (5:44)
> 2 Angie (4:24)
> 3 Smells Like Teen Spirit (3:17)
> 4 Thank You (3:52)

7" Single
East West A7504

> 1 Winter (5:44)
> 2 The Pool (2:51)

Cassette Single
East West A7504C

> 1 Winter (5:44)
> 2 The Pool (2:51)

Winter, the fourth UK *Little Earthquakes* single, was Tori's first of numerous CD singles to be released in a 2-part CD format. Part one includes the unreleased tracks *The Pool, Take To The Sky* and *Sweet Dreams*. Part two is a beautifully packaged limited edition picture CD including three cover versions of tracks that would become live favorites of Tori's, The Rolling Stones' *Angie*, Led Zeppelin's *Thank You* and especially Nirvana's *Smells Like Teen Spirit.*

UK Part 1 CD Single (Front)

UK Part 1 CD Single (Disc)

UK Part 1 CD Single (Back)

UK Part 2 CD Single (Front)

UK Part 2 CD Single (Disc)

UK Part 2 CD Single (Back)

UK 7" Single (Front)

UK 7" Single (Back)

UK 7" Single (A-Side)

UK 7" Single (B-Side)

UK Cassette Single

Winter (Germany)

CD Single
East West 85801
March 1992

> 1 Winter (5:40)
> 2 The Pool (2:49)
> 3 Smells Like Teen Spirit (3:15)

The German *Winter* CD single borrows *Winter* and *The Pool* from the UK *Winter* CD single part one and takes *Smells Like Teen Spirit* from the UK *Winter* part two CD single. Packaged in a slim jewel-case contrary to the UK jewel box and limited edition digipak.

German CD Single (Front)

German CD Single (Disc)

Winter (Australia)

CD Single
East West 85862-2
Released March 1992
Carboard Sleeve

Cassette Single
East West WEA 85862-4
Released March 1992

    1 Winter (5:40)
    2 Smells Like Teen Spirit (3:15)
    3 Angie (4:22)

Australian *Winter* CD single in a cardboard sleeve features the same tracks on the CD single and cassette single. This single features the same tracks as the UK *Winter* part two limited edition CD single with the exception of omitting *Thank You*.

Australian Cassette Single
(Front)

Australian Cassette Single
(Back)

Australian CD Single (Disc)

Australian CD Single (Front)

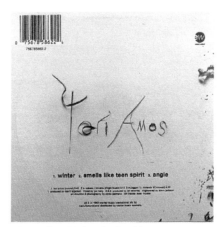

Australian CD Single (Back)

Silent All These Years (US)

Cassette Single
Atlantic 87511-4
April 1992

    1 Silent All These Years (4:11)
    2 Upside Down (4:22)

The first US post-*Y Kant Tori Read* single, *Silent All These Years*, was released commercially only as a cassette single in the US. It is backed with the unreleased *Upside Down* from the UK *Silent All These Years* single.

US Cassette Single (Front)

US Cassette Single (Back)

Silent All These Years (Japan)

3" CD Single
East West WMD5-4102
April 1992

    1 Silent All These Years (4:11)
    2 Me And A Gun (3:42)

One of the rarest *Little Earthquakes* singles, this obscure 2-track CD single was released in the now unusual 3" format in a 3" by 6" package with the lyrics printed on the back. Backed with *Me And A Gun*, it sold for 900 Yen, about $10 in 1992. Curiously, *Silent All These Years* has been the only single released to date in Japan.

Japanese 3" CD Single (Disc)

Japanese 3" CD Single (Front)

Japanese 3" CD Single (Back)

Crucify (US)

CD EP
Atlantic 82399-2
May 1992

Cassette EP Single
Atlantic 82399-4

    1 Crucify (Remix 4:18)
    2 Winter (5:44)
    3 Angie (4:26)
    4 Smells Like Teen Spirit (3:18)
    5 Thank You (3:49)

Cassette Single
Atlantic 87463-4

    1 Crucify (Remix 4:18)
    2 Me And A Gun (3:42)

Tori's first US CD single, a remixed *Crucify*, borrowed all four B sides from the UK *Winter* part two limited edition CD single and added *Me And A Gun* as the B side of the cassette single. There was also a cassette EP containing the same tracks as the CD single.

US CD EP (Front)

US CD EP (Back)

US Cassette EP Single
(Front)

US Cassette Single
(Front)

US Cassette Single (Back)

US CD EP (Long Box)

US CD EP (Disc)

Crucify (UK)

CD Single Part 1
East West A7479CD
June 1992

> 1 Crucify (Remix 4:18)
> 2 Here. in My Head (3:53)
> 3 Mary (4:27)
> 4 Crucify (LP Version 4:58)

CD Single Part 2 (Limited Edition CD EP Box)
East West A7479CDX

> 1 Little Earthquakes (Live 6:58)
> 2 Crucify (Live 5:19)
> 3 Precious Things (Live 5:03)
> 4 Mother (Live 6:37)

7" Single
East West A7479

Cassette Single
East West A7479C

> 1 Crucify (Remix 4:18)
> 2 Here. in My Head (3:53)

The fifth UK single from *Little Earthquakes* was originally scheduled to be a re-release of *Silent All These Years*, but in late May this was postponed in favor of *Crucify*. This turned out to be a fortuitous move as the remixed *Crucify* became Tori's highest charting single yet, peaking at number 15 and causing *Little Earthquakes* to re-enter the album charts.

Chart success was helped out by the release of the very limited edition *Crucify* Live EP Box containing four live tracks, *Little Earthquakes*, *Precious Things*, *Crucify* and *Mother* recorded April 5th, 1992 in Cambridge, England. The box also contained a set of four color prints of the covers of Tori's UK singles; *Silent All These Years*, *Winter*, *Crucify* and in place of *China*, the cover of *Little Earthquakes*, because that track is included on the EP. This live EP box is one of the most collectible and rare Tori items. Part one of the CD includes more non-LP tracks, the remixed version of *Crucify* (shortened from 4:58 to 4:15 and with guitar added) and the wonderful *Here. in My Head* and *Mary*. The *Crucify* (LP Version) as stated on part one is actually a slightly different mix from the actual LP version. It is about three seconds shorter, is more up-tempo and includes additional and different background vocals. The first pressing of the *Crucify* 7" misprinted "*Here. In My Hand*" on the label instead of *Here. in My Head* making this variation very collectible.

28

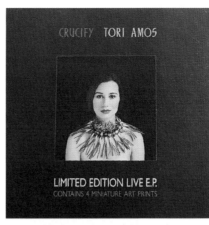

UK Part 1 CD Single (Front)

UK Part 2 Limited CD Single
Live EP Box (Front)

UK Part 2 Limited CD Single
Live EP Box (Back)

UK Cassette Single

UK 7" Single (Front)

UK 7" Single (Back)

UK 7" Single (A-Side) First Press

UK 7" Single (A-Side) Second Press

UK 7" Single (A-Side) East West

UK 7" Single (B-Side) First Press
with misprint

UK 7" Single (B-Side) Second Press

UK 7" Single (B-Side) East West

UK Part 2 CD Single Print (Little Earthquakes)

UK Part 2 Limited CD Single Print (Silent All TheseYears)

UK Part 2 Limited CD Single Print (Crucify)

UK Part 2 Limited CD Single Print (Winter)

UK Part 1 CD Single (Disc)

UK Part 2 Limited CD Single
Live EP (Disc)

Crucify (France)

French Cassette Single

CD Single
East West 87479
1992
Cardboard Sleeve

7" Single
East West 87479-7

Cassette Single
East West 87479-4

    1 Crucify (Remix 4:15)
    2 Here. in My Head (3:52)

The first of two *Crucify*
singles from France.
Packaged in a
cardboard sleeve, it
also includes *Here. in
My Head* from the UK
part one CD single.

French 7" Single (Front)

French CD Single (Front)

French CD Single (Disc)

French 7" Single (A-Side)

French CD Single (Back)

French 7" Single (B-Side)

2nd French CD Single (Front)

Crucify (France)

CD Single
Carrere/East West 85787
1992

> 1 Crucify (4:58)
> 2 Angie (4:22)
> 3 Smells Like Teen Spirit (3:15)

The second French *Crucify* single includes *Angie* and *Smells Like Teen Spirit*, originally appearing on the UK *Winter* part two CD single. This version of *Crucify* comes packaged in a thin jewel case.

Australian Cassette Single
(Front)

Crucify (Australia)

Cassette Single
East West 87479-4
19926

> 1 Crucify (4:15)
> 2 Here. in My Head (3:52)

Australian cassette single features the same tracks as the first French *Crucify* single.

Australian Cassette Single
(Back)

Silent All These Years (UK)

CD Single Part 1
East West A7433CD
August 1992

> 1 Silent All These Years (4:11)
> 2 Upside Down (4:22)
> 3 Me And A Gun (3:42)
> 4 Thoughts (2:36)

CD Single Part 2 (Limited Edition)
East West A7433CDX

> 1 Silent All These Years (4:12)
> 2 Ode To The Banana King (Part One) (4:06)
> 3 Song For Eric (1:50)
> 4 Happy Phantom (Live 3:33)

7" Single
East West A7433

Cassette Single
East West A7433C

> 1 Silent All These Years (4:11)
> 2 Smells Like Teen Spirit (3:15)

UK 7" Single Reissue (Front)

UK 7" Single Reissue (A-Side)

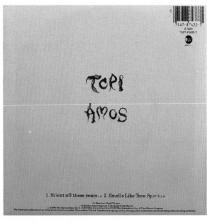

UK 7" Single Reissue (Back)

UK 7" Single Reissue (B-Side)

Postponed from May, *Silent All These Years* was finally re-released in August and became the sixth and final UK single from *Little Earthquakes*. *Silent All These Years* preserved the same tracks as the earlier *Me And A Gun* and *Silent All These Years* singles. However, the CD was no longer a picture disc, the CD insert no longer contained the lyrics of the earlier versions and the catalog numbers had been changed. The 7" single and cassette single replaced *Me And A Gun* with *Smells Like Teen Spirit* as the B side. Part two is a very limited CD single digipak that included the non-LP tracks *Ode To The Banana King (Part One)*, *Song For Eric* and a live version of *Happy Phantom*. The *Silent All These Years* limited CD single, along with the *Me And A Gun* CD single and the *Crucify* Live EP Box, are probably the three rarest commercial Tori CD singles.

UK Cassette Single (Front)

UK Cassette Single (Insert)

UK Part 1 CD Single Reissue (Front)

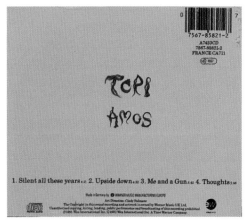

UK Part 1 CD Single Reissue (Back)

UK Part 1 CD Single Reissue (Disc)

UK Part 2 Limited CD Single (Front)

UK Part 2 Limited CD Single (Back)

UK Part 2 Limited CD Single (Disc)

Silent All These Years (Germany)

7" Single
East West 76013
1992

1 Silent All These Years (4:11)
2 Smells Like Teen Spirit (3:15)

German 7" Single (A-Side)

German 7" Single (B-Side)

US CD Single (Front)

US CD Single (Back)

US CD Single (Disc)

Winter (US)

CD Single
Atlantic 85799-2
November 1992

1 Winter (5:41)
2 The Pool (2:50)
3 Take To The Sky (4:17)
4 Sweet Dreams (3:26)
5 Upside Down (4:21)

Cassette Single
Atlantic 87418-4

1 Winter (Edit 4:38)
2 The Pool (2:50)

This beautiful digipak CD single includes reproductions of Tori's handwritten lyrics to all five tracks; the disc is a picture CD which is virtually identical to the US *Winter* 2-track promotional-only CD single. B sides are taken from the UK *Winter* part one CD single except for *Upside Down*, which first appeared on *Me And A Gun* and then on *Silent All These Years*. Until *Hey Jupiter* was released in 1996, *Winter* was probably the only US CD single that was more elaborately packaged than a UK single. The cover of the CD declares that it is a limited edition; however it is still relatively easy to find more than four years after its release. The cassette single contains an edited version of *Winter*, which, apart from this single, appears only on promotional copies.

US Cassette Single (Front)

US Cassette Single (Back)

Under The Pink

Cornflake Girl (UK)

CD Single Part 1
East West A7281CD
January 1994

> 1 Cornflake Girl (5:05)
> 2 Sister Janet (4:02)
> *Piano Suite*:
> > 3 All The Girls Hate Her (2:23)
> > 4 Over It (2:11)

CD Single Part 2 (Limited Edition)
East West A7281CDX

> 1 Cornflake Girl (5:05)
> 2 A Case Of You (4:38)
> 3 If 6 Was 9 (3:59)
> 4 Strange Fruit (4:00)

7" Single
East West A7281

> 1 Cornflake Girl (5:05)
> 2 Sister Janet (4:02)

Cassette Single
East West A7281C

> 1 Cornflake Girl (5:05)
> 2 Sister Janet (4:01)

Cornflake Girl, the first, by now intensely awaited new single, includes the unreleased *Sister Janet* and *Piano Suite*. Part two is one of the harder-to-find UK CD singles. This beautiful, limited edition picture CD is packaged in a fold-out digipak with a short statement from Tori regarding each of the three artists covered here. Two of these songs Tori used to play live in her early club days in Baltimore and Washington, Joni Mitchell's seductive *A Case Of You* and Billie Holiday's *Strange Fruit*, the latter having been recorded at 5:30 in the morning after Tori awoke to find "The Forces" bidding her to do so. A truly amazing version of Jimi Hendrix's *If 6 Was 9*—with Tori playing her piano through a Marshall amp—is also included. *Cornflake Girl* became Tori's highest charting UK single to date, reaching number four.

UK Part 1 CD Single (Front)

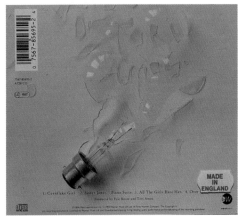

UK Part 1 CD Single (Back)

UK Part 1 CD Single (Disc)

UK Cassette Single (Front)

UK Part 2 Limited CD Single (Front)

UK Part 2 Limited CD Single (Back)

UK Part 2 Limited CD Single (Disc)

Cornflake Girl
(Germany)

7" Single
East West 87281-7

   1 Cornflake Girl (5:05)
   2 Sister Janet (4:02)

German 7" Single (A-Side)

German 7" Single (B-Side)

German 7" Single (Back)

UK 7" Single (Front)

UK 7" Single (A-Side)

UK 7" Single (B-Side)

Cornflake Girl (France)

CD Single
East West/Carrere Music 87281
1994

    1 Cornflake Girl (5:05)
    2 Sister Janet (4:01)
    Piano Suite:
      3 All The Girls Hate Her (2:23)
      4 Over It (2:11)

Cassette Single
East West/Carrere Music 87281-4

    1 Cornflake Girl (5:05)
    2 Sister Janet (4:01)

Cornflake Girl (Australia)

CD Single
East West 85695-2
February 1994
Cardboard Sleeve

    1 Cornflake Girl (5:05)
    2 Sister Janet (4:02)
    Piano Suite:
      3 All The Girls Hate Her (2:23)
      4 Over It (2:11)

Cassette Single
East West 87281-4

    1 Cornflake Girl (5:05)
    2 Sister Janet (4:02)

Australian package in the usual cardboard sleeve with slightly different packaging. Contains the same tracks as the UK part one CD single.

French CD Single (Front)

French Cassette Single

Australian Cassette Single

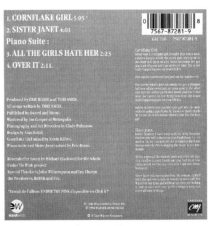

French CD Single (Back)

French CD Single (Disc)

Australian CD Single (Front)

Australian CD Single (Back)

US Cassette Single (Front)

US CD Single (Disc)

US CD Single (Front)

US CD Single (Back)

God (US)

CD Single
Atlantic 85687-2
February 1994

1 God (LP Version 3:58)
2 Home On The Range
(Cherokee Edition)
(5:25)
Piano Suite:
3 All The Girls
Hate Her (2:23)
4 Over It (2:11)

Cassette Single
Atlantic 87250-4

1 God (LP Version 3:58)
2 Sister Janet (4:02)

Under The Pink's first US single
and Tori's first number one
single, albeit on Billboard's
"Modern Rock Tracks" chart.
God includes *Piano Suite* from
the UK single of *Cornflake Girl*
and adds *Home On The Range*
(*Cherokee Edition*), an alteration
of the traditional version with
additional lyrics added by Tori.
God is packaged in a plastic and
cardboard case with a
completely different cover than
the UK version that would be
released six months later.
American radio was hesitant to
play *God* because of its too funky
and excessive (they thought)
guitar parts, so a 3-track
promotional-only single was
released with two remixed
versions of *God*, "No Guitar" and
"Some Guitar," as well as the
original album version.

God (Australia)

CD Single
East West 7567856872
August 1994
Cardboard Sleeve

1 God (LP Version 3:55)
2 Home On The Range (Cherokee Edition) (5:25)
 Piano Suite:
   3 All The Girls Hate Her (2:23)
   4 Over It (2:11)

Australian single in a cardboard sleeve features the same tracks as the US CD single with different artwork.

Australian Cassette Single
(Front)

Australian CD Single (Front)

Australian CD Single (Back)

Australian Cassette Single
(Back)

Australian CD Single (Disc)

Pretty Good Year (UK)

CD Single Part 1 (Limited Edition)
East West A7263CDX
March 1994

1 Pretty Good Year (3:25)
2 Home On The Range
 (Cherokee Edition) (5:26)
3 Daisy Dead Petals (3:02)

CD Single Part 2
East West A7263CD

1 Pretty Good Year (3:25)
2 Honey (3:47)
3 Black Swan (4:04)

7" Single
East West A7263

Cassette Single
East West A7263C

1 Pretty Good Year (3:25)
2 Honey (3:47)

UK Cassette Single

UK Part 1 Limited CD Single (Front)

UK Part 1 Limited CD Single (Disc)

Under The Pink's second UK single includes the non-LP *Daisy Dead Petals* and, taken from the US *God* single: *Home On The Range* (*Cherokee Edition*). This time, part one of the dual CD single release is the limited version, the disc is silver with honey coiled around the disc. The limited edition is a digipak with the lyrics to *Honey* printed on the center panel. Although *Honey* was not on this disc, it appeared on part two the following week.

Some part two singles feature black printing with a gold bee on the disc while others have a black bee and gold printing, so there are actually two versions of the part two single. Part two includes the superb non-LP track *Honey* as well as the

previously unreleased *Black Swan*. *Pretty Good Year* reached number seven in the UK. The limited *Pretty Good Year* is still relatively easy to find. *Honey* was originally scheduled to be included on *Under The Pink* but was left off because of lack of space.

FYI, for those wondering whatever happened to *Ode To The Banana King* "(*Part Two*)," Tori has stated that *Pretty Good Year* is part two and she will, at sometime in the future, deliver a part three.

UK Part 1 Limited CD Single (Back)

UK Part 2 CD Single (Front)

UK Part 2 CD Single (Gold Bee)

UK Part 2 CD Single (Back)

UK Part 2 CD Single (Black Bee)

UK 7" Single (Front)

UK 7" Single (Back)

UK 7" Single (A-Side)

UK 7" Single (B-Side)

Pretty Good Year (Australia)

CD Single
East West 85677-2
March 1994
Cardboard Sleeve

1 Pretty Good Year (3:25)
2 Honey (3:47)
3 Black Swan (4:04)

Cassette Single
East West 85677-4

1 Pretty Good Year (3:25)
2 Honey (3:47)
3 Black Swan (4:04)

Australian CD and cassette singles with the same tracks as the UK part two CD single. The CD single is packaged in a cardboard sleeve. The cassette single adds *Black Swan* as a third track, not fount on the UK cassette single.

Australian Cassette Single (Front)

Australian Cassette Single (Back)

Australian CD Single (Front)

Australian CD Single (Disc)

Australian CD Single (Back)

US CD Single (Front)

Cornflake Girl (US)

CD Single
Atlantic 85655-2
April 1994

    1 Cornflake Girl (Edit 3:53)
    2 Sister Janet (4:02)
    3 Daisy Dead Petals (3:02)
    4 Honey (3:47)

Cassette Single
Atlantic 87004-4

    1 Cornflake Girl (3:53)
    2 Honey (3:47)

US CD Single (Back)

The US version of *Cornflake Girl*, in a plastic and
cardboard package, featured a completely
different and unique cover from the earlier
Cornflake Girl UK singles. The non-LP *Daisy
Dead Petals* and *Honey* were taken from the UK
Pretty Good Year singles while *Sister Janet* had
appeared on the UK *Cornflake Girl* part one
single.

US CD Single (Disc)

US Cassette Single (Front)

US Cassette Single (Back)

Past The Mission (UK)

UK Part 1 Limited CD Single (Front)

UK Part 1 Limited CD Single (Back)

UK Part 1 Limited CD Single (Back Panel)

CD Single Part 1 (Limited Edition)
East West A7257CDX
May 1994

    1 Upside Down (Live 5:57)
    2 Past The Mission (Live 4:21)
    3 Icicle (Live 7:50)
    4 Flying Dutchman (Live 6:31)

CD Single Part 2
East West A7257CD

    1 Past The Mission (LP Version 4:05)
    2 Winter (Live 6:37)
    3 The Waitress (Live 3:29)
    4 Here. in My Head (Live 6:05)

7" Single
East West A7257

Cassette Single
East West A7257C

    1 Past The Mission (LP Version 4:05)
    2 Past The Mission (Live 4:21)

The third UK *Under The Pink* single, *Past The Mission*, includes seven live tracks as the B sides between two singles. Recorded in the US and the UK during March 1994: *Upside Down* live in Boston March 31st, *Past The Mission* and *Flying Dutchman* live in Chicago March 24th, *Icicle* live in Los Angeles March 22nd, *Winter* live in Manchester March 1st, *The Waitress* live in Boston March 31st and *Here. in My Head* live in Bristol March 7th. Part one is a limited edition fold-out digipak including February to May 1994 tour dates on the center panel. *Past The Mission*, while limited, is one of the easier to find UK singles. Worth noting: the UK *Past The Mission* part two CD single is a reverse picture CD while the German pressing is a positive photographic image.

UK Part 1 Limited CD Single (Disc)

UK 7" Single (A-Side)

UK 7" Single (B-Side)

Past The Mission (Germany)

CD Single
East West 85644-2
May 1994

1 Past The Mission (LP Version 4:05)
2 Winter (Live 6:37)
3 The Waitress (Live 3:29)
4 Here. in My Head (Live 6:05)

German *Past The Mission* CD single features the same tracks as the UK part two CD single. The principal difference between the two CD singles is that the UK version has a reverse photographic image of Tori on the disc while the German version has a positive image. The UK promotional-only CD single of *Past The Mission* also has the positive photographic image.

UK Part 2 CD Single (Front)

UK Part 2 CD Single (Back)

UK Part 2 CD Single (Disc)

UK 7" Single (Front)

UK 7" Single (Back)

German CD Single (Back)

German CD Single (Disc)

Past The Mission (US)

Cassette Single
Atlantic 87206-4
1994

    1 Past The Mission (4:05)
    2 Black Swan (4:04)

Past The Mission was released commercially only as a cassette single in the US but was issued as a limited edition promotional-only single. The non-LP *Black Swan* was taken from the UK part two *Pretty Good Year*.

US Cassette Single (Front)   US Cassette Single (Back)

Past The Mission (Australia)

CD Single
East West 756785664-2
1994
Cardboard Sleeve

    1 Past The Mission (LP Version 4:05)
    2 Winter (Live 6:37)
    3 The Waitress (Live 3:29)
    4 Here. in My Head (Live 6:05)

Cassette Single
East West 756785664-4

    1 Past The Mission (LP Version 4:05)
    2 Past The Mission (Live 4:21)

Australian CD single in a cardboard sleeve with the same track listing as the UK part two CD single.

Australian Cassette Single (Front)

Australian CD Single (Front)

Australian Cassette Single (Back)

Australian CD Single (Disc)

God (UK)

CD Single
East West A7251CD
August 1994

   1 God (3:58)
   2 God (The Dharma Kayâ Mix 12:34)
   3 God (The Rainforest Resort Mix 10:32)
   4 God (The Thinking Mix 2 9:50)

12" Single
East West A7251T

   1 God (The Thinking Mix 2 9:50)
   2 God (Acapella Vocal and Rain Mix 4:42)
   3 God (The Rainforest Resort Mix 10:32)
   4 God (The CJ Bolland Mix 5:58)

7" Picture Disc
East West A7251-P

Cassette Single
East West A7251C

   1 God (3:58)
   2 God (Acapella Vocal and Rain Mix 4:42)

The fourth and final UK single from *Under The Pink* had a few interesting variations. It was released in three formats: CD single, 12" single (the first since *China*) and a beautiful 7" picture disc. In addition, the 12" and CD single had tracks unique to them. The CD single had *God* (*The Dharma Kayâ Mix*) exclusively while the 12" had *God* (*The CJ Bolland Mix*) to itself. The 7", 12" and cassette single shared *God* (*Acapella Vocal* and *Rain Mix*) while the CD single and 12" shared *God* (*The Thinking Mix 2*).

UK CD Single (Disc)

UK CD Single (Front)

UK CD Single (Back)

UK 12" Single (Front)

UK 12" Single (Back)

UK 12" Single (A-Side)

UK 12" Single (B-Side)

UK 7" Single (Insert)

UK 7" Single Picture Disc (A-Side)

UK 7" Single Picture Disc (B-Side)

UK Cassette Single

God (Germany)

CD Single
East West 85637
August 1994

1 God (3:58)
2 God (The Dharma Kayâ Mix 12:34)
3 God (The Rainforest Resort Mix 10:32)
4 God (The Thinking Mix 2 9:50)

The German *God* single included the same tracks as the UK version although omitting the beautiful color shot of Tori on the back of the insert. Packaged in a thin case as compared to the UK jewel box.

German CD Single (Front)

German CD Single (Disc)

Boys For Pele

Caught A Lite Sneeze (UK)

CD Single Part 1
East West A5524CD1
January 1996

> 1 Caught A Lite Sneeze (4:24)
> *Silly Songs*:
>> 2 This Old Man (1:44)
>> 3 Hungarian Wedding Song (1:00)
>> 4 Toodles Mr. Jim (3:09)

CD Single Part 2 (Limited Edition)
East West A5524CD2

> 1 Caught A Lite Sneeze (4:24)
> *Tribute to Chas and Dave*:
>> 2 London Girls (3:20)
>> 3 That's What I Like Mick
>>   (The Sandwich Song) (2:59)
>> 4 Samurai (3:03)

Cassette Single
East West A5524C

> 1 Caught A Lite Sneeze (4:24)
> 2 Graveyard (0:55)
> 3 Toodles Mr. Jim (3:09)

The first *Boys For Pele* UK singles had some curious B sides. The non-LP cover versions of *This Old Man*, *London Girls*[†] and *That's What I Like Mick* (*The Sandwich Song*) as well as new unreleased Tori songs *Hungarian Wedding Song*, *Toodles Mr. Jim*, *Samurai* and *Graveyard*.

The haunting *Graveyard* is only found on the cassette single and *Toodles Mr. Jim* was added to the Japanese CD version of *Boys For Pele* as a bonus track. *Graveyard* would turn up later on the US and French *Caught A Lite Sneeze* CD singles. *Caught A Lite Sneeze* peaked at number 20 in the UK. The part two limited edition digipak contained a beautiful picture CD of a portion of the cover shot. No vinyl was released for *Caught A Lite Sneeze*.

[†]*Tori played a passionate version of* London Girls *to a very enthusiastic crowd at her Royal Albert Hall show in London, March 8th, 1996.*

UK Part 1 CD Single (Front)

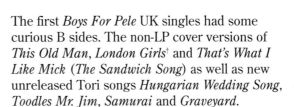
UK Part 1 CD Single (Back)

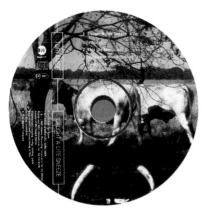
UK Part 1 CD Single (Disc)

UK Cassette Single

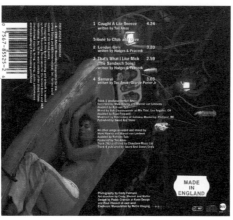

UK Part 2 Limited CD Single (Front)　　　　UK Part 2 Limited CD Single (Back)　　　　UK Part 2 Limited CD Single (Disc)

Caught A Lite Sneeze (US)

CD Single
Atlantic 85519-2
January 1996

1　Caught A Lite Sneeze
　　(Unedited Version 4:26)
　　Silly Songs:
　　2　This Old Man (1:44)
　　3　That's What I Like Mick
　　　　(The Sandwich Song) (2:59)
　　4　Graveyard (0:55)
　　5　Toodles Mr. Jim (3:09)

The first US single from *Boys For Pele*, also *Caught A Lite Sneeze,* added *Graveyard* from the UK cassette single and borrowed tracks from both parts of the UK CD singles omitting *London Girls, Samurai* and *Hungarian Wedding Song. Caught A Lite Sneeze* entered the US charts at number 70, peaked at number 60 then disappeared. Packaged in a thin jewel-case, the US version, unlike the UK singles, is not a picture CD.

US CD Single (Front)

US CD Single (Back)

US CD Single (Disc)

50

Caught A Lite Sneeze (Australia)

CD Single
East West 756785526-2
February 1996
Cardboard Sleeve

    1 Caught A Lite Sneeze (4:24)
      Silly Songs:
        2 This Old Man (1:44)
        3 Hungarian Wedding Song (1:00)
        4 Toodles Mr. Jim (3:09)

Cassette Single
East West 756785524-4

    1 Caught A Lite Sneeze (4:24)
    2 Graveyard (0:54)
    3 Toodles Mr. Jim (3:09)

Australian version duplicates the UK CD single part one track listing but comes packaged in a cardboard sleeve with a black border and black, white and silver picture CD. The cassette single adds *Graveyard*, found also on the US and French *Caught A Lite Sneeze* CD singles and UK cassette single.

Australian Cassette Single
(Front)

Australian Cassette Single
(Back)

Australian CD Single (Front)

Australian CD Single (Disc)

Australian CD Single (Back)

Caught A Lite Sneeze (France)

CD Single
East West 85524-2
February 1996
Cardboard Sleeve

    1 Caught A Lite Sneeze (4:24)
    2 Graveyard (0:54)
    3 Toodles Mr. Jim (3:09)

French *Caught A Lite Sneeze* CD single duplicates the track listing from the UK cassette single. *Graveyard* appears on CD here for only the second time, the first being the US *Caught A Lite Sneeze* CD single. Packaged in a cardboard sleeve.

French CD Single (Front)

French CD Single (Disc)

Caught A Lite Sneeze (Germany)

CD Single Part 1
East West 85526-2
February 1996

1 Caught A Lite Sneeze (4:24)
Silly Songs:
2 This Old Man (1:44)
3 Hungarian Wedding Song (1:00)
4 Toodles Mr. Jim (3:09)

CD Single Part 2 (Limited Edition)
East West 85525-2
February 1996

1 Caught A Lite Sneeze (4:24)
Tribute to Chas and Dave:
2 London Girls (3:20)
3 That's What I Like Mick
(The Sandwich Song) (2:59)
4 Samurai (3:03)

German *Caught A Lite Sneeze* singles duplicate tracks from the UK versions although the German part two limited edition single comes in a slim jewel-case as compared with the UK Version which is a digipak. The German part two *Caught A Lite Sneeze* CD single is a black and white picture disc as compared with the beautiful UK color disc.

German Part 1 CD Single (Disc)

German Part 1 CD Single (Front)

German Part 2 Limited CD Single (Front)

German Part 2 Limited CD Single (Back)

Talula (UK)

CD Single Part 1
East West A8512CD1
March 1996

> 1 Talula (The Tornado Mix 3:43)
> 2 Talula (BT's Synethasia Mix 11:27)
> 3 Amazing Grace/Til' The Chicken (6:48)

CD Single Part 2
East West A8512CD2
March 1996

> 1 Talula (The Tornado Mix 3:43)
> 2 Frog On My Toe (3:40)
> 3 Sister Named Desire (5:29)
> 4 Alamo (5:11)

Cassette Single
East West A8512C

> 1 Talula (The Tornado Mix 3:43)
> 2 Sister Named Desire (5:29)

The second pair of UK singles from *Boys For Pele* include more unreleased tracks, part one features a remix of *Talula* (*The Tornado Mix*), *Talula* (*BT's Synethasia Mix*) followed by *Amazing Grace/Til' The Chicken*. Part two includes three new Tori songs, *Frog On My Toe*, *Sister Named Desire* and *Alamo*. With *Til' The Chicken*, Tori is making light of an incident that took place during the recording of *Past The Mission* at Trent Reznor's house in Los Angeles. At the time of the recording, Trent lived in the actual house where Sharon Tate and four others were murdered in 1969. During a break in the recording, Tori attempted to cook a chicken in the oven but the chicken would not cook, even after hours in the oven. Tori is sure that it had something to do with the lingering spirits in the house. *Talula* is the first 2-part UK single where neither part is a limited edition. Like *Caught A Lite Sneeze* there was no vinyl for *Talula*.

UK Part 1 CD Single (Front)

UK Part 1 CD Single (Disc)

UK Part 1 CD Single (Back)

UK Cassette Single

UK Part 2 CD Single (Front)

UK Part 2 CD Single (Disc)

UK Part 2 CD Single (Back)

Talula (US)

CD Single
Atlantic 85504
May 1996

1 Talula (Tornado Album Version 3:43)
2 Samurai (3:03)
3 Frog On My Toe (3:40)
4 London Girls (3:20)
5 Talula (BT's Synethasia Mix 11:27)

Talula (Australia)

CD Single
East West 88512
April 1996
Cardboard Sleeve

1 Talula (The Tornado Mix 3:43)
2 Talula (BT's Synethasia Mix 11:27)
3 Amazing Grace/Til' The Chicken (6:48)

US CD Single (Front)

Second US single from *Boys For Pele* borrows *London Girls* and *Samurai* from the UK *Caught A Lite Sneeze* part two CD single, *Frog On My Toe* from the UK *Talula* part two CD single and *Talula* (*BT's Synethasia Mix*) from the UK *Talula* part one CD single. *Talula*, the title track, is named *Tornado Album Version* here but called *Tornado Mix* in the UK and Australia.

Australian CD Single (Front)

US CD Single (Disc)

Australian CD Single (Disc)

US CD Single (Back)

Professional Widow (US)

CD Single
Atlantic 85499-2
July 1996

1 Professional Widow
   (LP Mix 4:31)
2 Professional Widow
   (Armand's Star Trunk Funkin' Mix 8:08)
3 Professional Widow
   (MK Mix 7:20)
4 Professional Widow
   (Just Da Funk Dub 3:44)
5 Professional Widow
   (MK Vampire Dub 6:56)
6 Professional Widow
   (Armand's Instrumental 5:35)
7 Professional Widow
   (Bonus Beats 4:31)

12" Single
Atlantic 0-85499

1 Professional Widow
   (Armand's Star Trunk Funkin' Mix 8:08)
2 Professional Widow
   (Just Da Funk Dub 3:44)
3 Professional Widow
   (MK Mix 7:20)
4 Professional Widow
   (MK Vampire Dub 6:56)

US 12" Single (Front)

US 12" Single (Back)

US 12" Single (A-Side)

US 12" Single (B-Side)

The third US *Boys For Pele* single was Tori's first release targeted for club play and her first US 12" release ever. (Not counting the promotional-only 12" of *The Big Picture* in 1988). The 12" and CD contain gorgeous artwork of a radiant Tori. There was a promotional poster released just prior to the single featuring a shot from the same session. Atlantic correctly predicted a number one club hit in June when an advance promotional 12" was serviced to clubs. Remixes were done by Armand Van Helden and MK, two of the premier underground producers of the moment. The 12" entered the Billboard "Dance/Club play" chart at number 37 and four weeks later on July 27th, reached number one and stayed there for two weeks. This was Tori's second number one single, the first being *God* ("Modern Rock Tracks" chart). Although *Professional Widow* hit number one on the "Dance/Club play" chart, it only reached number 108 on the Billboard "Top 200 Singles" chart. The CD single clocks in at over forty minutes and contains six remixes of *Professional Widow* as well as the LP version. The 12" contains four remixes. The commercial 12" contains exactly the same tracks as the white-sleeved promotional 12" released in June.

US CD Single (Front)

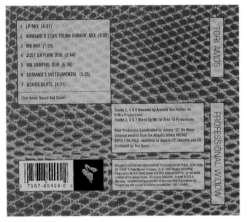

US CD Single (Back)

US CD Single (Disc)

Hey Jupiter/ Professional Widow(UK)

CD Single
East West A5494CD
July 1996

1 Hey Jupiter (The Dakota Version 6:03)
2 Professional Widow
   (Armand's Star Trunk Funkin' Mix)
   (Radio Edit 3:45)
3 Sugar (Live 5:43)
4 Honey (Live 4:19)

12" Single
East West A5494T

1 Professional Widow
   (Armand's Star Trunk Funkin' Mix 8:08)
2 Hey Jupiter
   (The Dakota Version)
   (Radio Edit 4:14)
3 Talula (B.T.'s Synethasia Mix 11:27)

Cassette Single
East West A5494C

1 Hey Jupiter (Dakota Version 6:03)
2 Professional Widow
   (Armand's Star Trunk Funkin' Mix)
   (Radio Edit 3:45)

Hey Jupiter was released in the UK as a double A side single. The CD leads off with *Hey Jupiter* (*Dakota Version*), a wonderfully slow and somewhat industrial remix, while the 12" (The first vinyl single released in the UK from *Boys For Pele*) features *Professional Widow* as the A side. *Professional Widow* entered the UK Dance Charts at number one and the singles chart at number 20, the highest position yet of any *Boys For Pele* single. The CD contains a radio edit of the remixed *Professional Widow* as well as newly recorded live versions of *Sugar* and *Honey*. The 12" contains an edited version of *Hey Jupiter* that is not found on the commercial CD single, but is found on the US promotional-only CD single. Also included is the long (11:27) remixed version of *Talula*. The CD insert contains a color shot of Tori that is actually a slightly different photo from the picture the cover was taken from. The disc itself is a picture CD. *Hey Jupiter* was the first UK single since *God* that was not released as a 2-part CD single. The timing of *Sugar* is incorrectly stated as 5:43; it is actually 5:33 and would appear correctly on the US release the following month.

UK CD Single (Front)

UK 12" Single (Front)

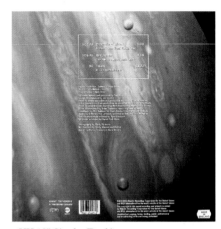

UK 12" Single (Back)

UK CD Single (Back)

UK CD Single (Disc)

UK 12" Single (A-Side)

UK 12" Single (B-Side)

UK Cassette Single

Hey Jupiter (US)

CD Single EP
Atlantic 82955-2
August 1996

1 Hey Jupiter (Dakota Version 6:03)
2 Sugar (Live 5:33)
3 Honey (Live 4:19)
4 Professional Widow
   (Merry Widow Version Live 4:38)
5 Somewhere Over The Rainbow
   (Live 4:31)

US CD Single (Front)

US CD Single (Back)

Hey Jupiter (Dakota Version) leads off the US EP. A shortened (3:55) version of this track is featured in the US promotional video instead of the album version. This same track can be found on the UK *Hey Jupiter/ Professional Widow* single as well as on the US *Hey Jupiter* promotional-only CD single. The EP contains Tori's superb live cover of *Over The Rainbow*[†], which was not included on the UK version released in July. The US version also replaces *Professional Widow (Armand's Star Trunk Funkin' Mix)(Edit)*, from the UK single, with a live version of *Professional Widow*

called *Merry Widow Version*. The US EP borrows the live versions of *Sugar* and *Honey* from the UK single. *Hey Jupiter* was released only on CD in the US and packaged in a beautiful three panel digipak containing a picture CD. With the inclusion of the live versions of *Over The Rainbow* and *Professional Widow*, as well as the elaborate packaging, the US version is considerably more desirable than the UK single.

[†] *Over The Rainbow is actually the correct title of this track; Atlantic incorrectly printed it as Somewhere Over The Rainbow on the single.*

US CD Single (Disc)

In The Springtime Of His Voodoo (US)

CD Single
Atlantic 85475-2
September 1996

1 In The Springtime Of His Voodoo
   (LP Mix 5:32)
2 In The Springtime Of His Voodoo
   (Hasbrouck Heights Single Mix 4:25)
3 In The Springtime Of His Voodoo
   (Hasbrouck Heights Club Mix 10:04)
4 In The Springtime Of His Voodoo
   (Quiet Mix 4:30)
5 In The Springtime Of His Voodoo
   (Sugar Dub 8:52)

12" Single
Atlantic 0-85475

1 In The Springtime Of His Voodoo
   (Hasbrouck Heights Club Mix 10:00)
2 In The Springtime Of His Voodoo
   (Quiet Mix 4:24)
3 In The Springtime Of His Voodoo
   (Sugar Dub 8:53)
4 In The Springtime Of His Voodoo
   (Hasbrouck Heights Single Mix 4:22)

US 12" Single (Front)

US 12" Single (Back)

Following on the heels of the number one club hit *Professional Widow* comes another remix EP meant for the clubs. *In The Springtime Of His Voodoo* is produced by Vinnie Vero and Steve Donato, the former having previously worked with Gloria Estafan and Deep Forest. Released again in both 12" and CD single formats, the track listing of the two formats differs only slightly. The CD single contains one track not found on the 12": the LP Mix. In their pre-release sheets, Atlantic declares "Newly appointed dance-diva Tori Amos hits the club circuit again…." The 12" entered the "Dance/Club" play charts at number 39 and peaked at number six after six weeks.

US 12" Single (A-Side)

US 12" Single (B-Side)

US CD Single (Front)

US CD Single (Back)

US CD Single (Disc)

chapter three
promotional items

Y Kant Tori Read (US)

LP Test Pressing
Atlantic 81845-1
June 1988

Atlantic white label test pressing of *Y Kant Tori Read* issued prior to the album's release is one of the rarest Tori items ever made. Note: misspelling of name on the label.

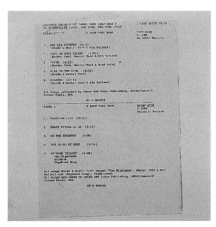

US LP Test Pressing (Front)

US LP Test Pressing (A-Side)

US LP Test Pressing (B-Side)

Y Kant Tori Read

The Big Picture (US)

7" Single
Atlantic 89086
June 1988

12" Single
Atlantic PR2298

1 The Big Picture (4:19)
2 The Big Picture (4:19)

Very rare double A side promotional-only singles released prior to *Y Kant Tori Read* in 1988. The picture sleeve 12" is Tori's first, and the last US 12" until *Professional Widow* was released in July, 1996.

US Promo 7" Single (A-Side)

US Promo 7" Single (B-Side)

US Promo 12" Single (Front)

US Promo 12" Single (Back)

US Promo 12" Single (Label)

Cool On Your Island (US)

7" Single
Atlantic 7-89021
June 1988

   1 Cool On Your Island (Edit 4:05)
   2 Cool On Your Island (Edit 4:05)

CD Single
Atlantic PR2452

   1 Phil Collins: A Groovy Kind of Love
   2 Cool On Your Island (Edit 4:05)
   3 Cool On Your Island (LP Version 4:57)

US Promo CD Single (Back)

Tori's first CD single was a promotional-only release which *Y Kant Tori Read* shared with Atlantic label-mate Phil Collins. The CD single included both the LP version and edited version of *Cool On Your Island*. The 7" is a double A side featuring an edited version of *Cool On Your Island*.

US Promo 7" Single (Front)

US Promo CD (Disc)

Little Earthquakes

Tori Amos (UK)

Cassette Sampler
East West (July 1991)

    1 Winter (5:45)
    2 Crucify (4:59)
    3 Silent All These Years (4:13)
    4 Leather (3:14)

The earliest *Little Earthquakes* promotional-only item was this 4-track cassette sampler distributed by East West Records UK in July 1991, three months before *Me And A Gun* was released as the first single.

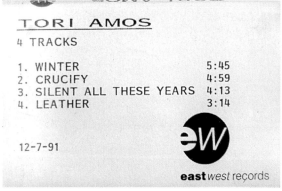

UK Promotional Cassette Sampler

Silent All These Years (UK)

10" Test Pressing Acetate Single
East West
October 1991

    1 Silent All These Years (Faded) (4:10)

UK promotional-only 1-sided acetate is actually a 7" single cut into a 10" disc. This was sent to radio stations in October, 1991 and instantly became one of the rarest Tori records ever released.

UK 10" Acetate Test Pressing (Sleeve)

UK 10" Acetate Test Pressing (Disc)

Silent All These Years (UK)

7" Single
East West YZ618DJ
October 1991

   1 Silent All These Years (4:13)
   2 Upside Down (4:22)

Silent All These Years
UK promotional 7"
features the sleeve
from *Me And A Gun*
but the record plays
Silent All These Years.
To add further
confusion, the B side is
listed as *Thoughts* but
the record actually
plays *Upside Down.*

Little Earthquakes (UK)

Cassette
East West
December 1991

UK East West Records advance promotional-only
cassettes, the first and rarest version includes
Flying Dutchman as the 13th track, which was
originally intended to be included on *Little
Earthquakes. Flying Dutchman* was later removed
from the album because of its length and later
appeared as a B side of *China.* The album was re-
sequenced moving *Little Earthquakes* from track
seven to close the album as the 12th and final
track. The second version is an advance copy of
the album as it was finally released.

UK 13-Track Advance
Cassette (Front and Spine)

UK Promo 7" Single (Front)

UK Promo 7" Single (A-side)

UK 12-Track Advance
Cassette (Front)

UK Promo 7" Single (Back)

UK Promo 7" Single (B-side)

65

Little Earthquakes (US)

Cassette
Atlantic 82358-4A
December 1991

Atlantic 82358-4
January 1991

The ultra-rare US advance promotional-only cassette release features a black and white cover shot of Tori, the track listing remained the same as the released version. The later, color promotional copies have the spine of the tape printed to declare that they are indeed "Promotional." This was done on all Atlantic cassettes through the early 1990s. The promotional cassette of *Y Kant Tori Read* has a similar spine.

US Advance Promo Cassette

US Promo Cassette
(Front and Spine)

China (UK)

CD Single
East West A7531CDDJ
January 1992

    1 China (Edit 3:35)
    2 Sugar (4:27)
    3 Flying Dutchman (6:31)
    4 Humpty Dumpty (2:52)

7" Single
East West A7531DJ

    1 China (Edit 3:35)
    2 China (5:01)

UK promotional CD single and 7" include the rare edited version of *China*.

UK Promo 7" Single (Front)

UK Promo 7" Single (Back)

UK Promo 7" Single (A-Side)

UK Promo 7" Single (B-Side)

Silent All These Years (US)

CD Single
Atlantic PRCD 4454-2
1992

    1 Silent All These Years (4:10)

The first *Little Earthquakes* US single was the 1-track promotional-only CD single version of *Silent All These Years*.

US Promo CD Single (Front)

US Promo CD Single (Disc)

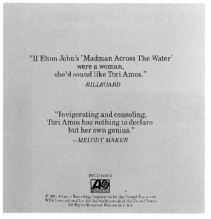

US Promo CD Single (Insert Back)

US Promo CD Single (Back)

US Promo CD Single #1 (Front)

Crucify (US)

CD Single
Atlantic PRCD 4598-2
1992

    1 Crucify (Remix 4:15)

US 1-track *Crucify* promotional-only CD single was released with two variations. The first version features a sticker on the jewel box, the second includes an actual insert with much brighter and clearer graphics.

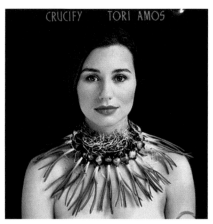

US Promo CD Single #2 (Front)

Precious Things (US)

CD Single Picture Disc
Atlantic PRCD 4742-2
1992

    1 Precious Things (4:26)
    2 Upside Down (4:22)
    3 Flying Dutchman (6:31)
    4 Mary (4:27)
    5 Mother (Live 6:42)

US Promo CD Single (Disc)

Atlantic did consider and eventually abandon the idea of a commercial *Precious Things* release, instead issuing this very limited and beautiful promotional-only picture CD including four B sides. The rarest US promotional-only single.

US Promo CD Single (Back)

US Promo CD Single (Back)

US Promo CD Single (Disc)

Silent All These Years (UK)

CD Single
East West A7433CDDJ
August 1992

    1 Silent All These Years (4:11)
    2 Smells Like Teen Spirit (3:15)

UK 2-track promotional-only CD single in a slim jewel-case. The sleeve and disc denotes that this is a promotional copy.

UK Promo CD Single (Front)

UK Promo CD Single (Disc)

Winter (US)

CD Single Picture Disc
Atlantic PRCD 4800-2
1992

    1 Winter (Edit 4:38)
    2 Winter (LP Version 5:41)

2-track promotional-only picture CD of *Winter* is similar to the UK *Winter* part two disc except the US CD has a silver background while the UK version is a more attractive white background. Since the LP version of *Winter* is almost six minutes long, this CD was released with a 4:38 edited version.

US Promo CD Single (Back)

US Promo CD Single (Disc)

Little Earthquakes: Tour Souvenir (Australia)

Cassette
East West TA-1
November 1992

    1 Little Earthquakes (Live 6:58)
    2 Crucify (Live 5:19)
    3 Smells Like Teen Spirit (3:17)
    4 Angie (4:24)
    5 Precious Things (Live 5:03)
    6 Mother (Live 6:37)

Beautiful Australian cassette sampler borrows the live tracks from the UK *Crucify* Live EP and adds *Angie* and *Smells Like Teen Spirit* from the Australian *Winter* CD single. This cassette was included free with the Australian *Little Earthquakes* video for a short time to coincide with the 1992 tour.

Australian Tour Souvenir Cassette (Front)

Australian Tour Souvenir Cassette (Back)

Little Drummer Boy (UK)

CD Single
East West
December 1992

    1 Little Drummer Boy (3:20)

Recordable CD-R issued to UK Radio in December 1992, one full year before *Little Drummer Boy* was issued as a US promotional-only CD in December 1993. Easily one of the very rarest Tori items in existence.

UK Promo CD-R (Front and Spine)

UK Promo CD-R (Disc)

Little Drummer Boy (US)

CD Single
Atlantic PRCD 5409
December 1993

    1 Little Drummer Boy (Live 3:20)

Recorded November 11th 1992 at Steeltown, Baltimore, MD USA. Silver CD in a jewel box with name and title only, no insert. This was one of the rarest promotional CDs for two years until it appeared on two different Atlantic promotional-only Christmas samplers, *You Sleigh Me* and *So This Is Christmas*. *Little Drummer Boy* next appeared on the 2-CD Australian *Under The Pink* and *More Pink* collection. Atlantic devalued it further by releasing a different version of *You Sleigh Me* commercially in November 1995 which also contains *Little Drummer Boy*. Prior to these releases, the only other way to obtain it was on the hard-to-find "We've Got Your Yule Logs Hangin'" KROQ charity cassette. This CD is still quite rare and very hard to find.

US Promo CD Single (Back)

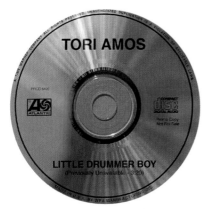

US Promo CD Single (Disc)

Under The Pink (US)

CD
Atlantic PRCD 5397-2
December 1993

The *Under The Pink* advance CD was originally intended to be released in a digipak; however Tori did not approve of the cover photo, hence, almost all covers were destroyed. The white CD was then placed in a jewel box with no insert. Track listing remained the same as the released version. The advance digipak is the rarest Tori CD in existence; only a few copies are known to exist, making it unobtainable.

Cassette
Atlantic PR5397-4
December 1993

The advance promotional-only cassette was also shipped without a cover because these were destroyed as well. A small quantity were shipped with the unauthorized cover intact. This is now one of the rarest collector's items.

Cassette
Atlantic 82567
December 1993

The advance promotional cassette version that was finally released after the original version was scrapped.

DAT

Advance release DAT sent out November 15th, 1993, on the final day of mastering of *Under The Pink*.

US Advance Promo CD Digipak (Front)

US Advance Promo CD Digipak (Back and Spine)

US Advance Promo CD Digipak (Disc)

US Advance Promo Cassette
(Front and Spine)

UK Advance Promo Cassette
(Front and Spine)

Hong Kong Advance Promo CD

US Advance
Promo Cassette
(Rare Cover Front)

US Advance Promo
Cassette (Rare Cover
Back and Spine)

TORI AMOS
"Under The Pink"

SIDE A
1. Pretty Good Year
2. God
3. Bells For Her
4. Past The Mission
5. Baker Baker
6. The Wrong Band
7. The Waitress
SIDE B
1. Cornflake Girl
2. Icicle
3. Cloud On My Tongue
4. Space Dog
5. Yes, Anastasia

WARNER MUSIC CANADA

Canadian Advance Promo
Cassette (Front and Spine)

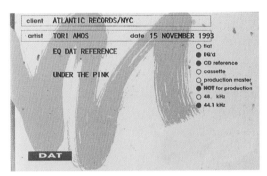

client ATLANTIC RECORDS/NYC
artist TORI AMOS   date 15 NOVEMBER 1993
EQ DAT REFERENCE
○ flat
● EQ'd
● CD reference
○ cassette
UNDER THE PINK
○ production master
● NOT for production
○ 48 kHz
● 44.1 kHz

DAT

US Advance DAT (Box)

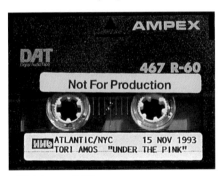

US Advance DAT

Tori Amos Sampler (UK)

Cassette
East West TA-1
December 1993

1 Pretty Good Year (3:25)
2 God (3:58)
3 Bells For Her (5:20)
4 Cornflake Girl (5:06)
5 Past The Mission (4:05)

Black and white UK promotional-only sampler of selected tracks from *Under The Pink* shipped before the album's release in January 1994. Extremely rare.

UK Promo Cassette (Front)

UK Promo Cassette (Back)

Under The Pink (France)

French Promo
Plastic Box/CD/Video
Carrere Music/East West
1994

In 1992, Carrere/East West in France issued the *Little Earthquakes* promotional-only wooden box which instantly became one of the most sought-after Tori collectibles. In 1994, Carrere/East West issued this unique clear plastic box containing the German *Under The Pink* CD as well as a promotional video for *Cornflake Girl* (UK Version). The video comes in a beautiful sleeve with the artwork from the French *Cornflake Girl* CD single. The box also includes a promotional biography printed in French. The *Under The Pink* plastic box is even more difficult to find than the *Little Earthquakes* wooden box.

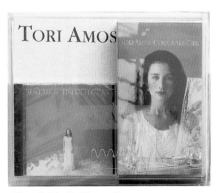

French Plastic Promo Box

Under The Pink
(Germany)

German Promo CD
East West/Atlantic
January 1994

German advance promotional CD for *Under The Pink* in a special folder announcing the release date of January 28th 1994 and the beginning of the German *Under The Pink* tour the following April.

German Promo CD (Front)

German Promo CD (Back)

German Promo CD (Inside)

Cornflake Girl
(UK)

CD Single
East West A7281CDDJ
December 1993

1 Cornflake Girl (Edit 3:53)
2 Sister Janet (4:02)
   Piano Suite:
   3 All The Girls Hate Her (2:23)
   4 Over It (2:11)

Thin jewel case with the same tracks as the UK CD single of *Cornflake Girl* part one, except here *Cornflake Girl* is the edited version, which is 1:12 shorter and which also appears on the US CD single. Note Tori's red hair on the disc.

UK Promo CD Single (Front)

UK Promo CD Single (Disc)

Cornflake Girl (US)

CD Single
Atlantic PRCD 5606-2
1994

1 Cornflake Girl (Edit 3:53)
2 Cornflake Girl
  (Album Version 5:06)

US 2-track promotional-only CD single in a jewel box with the same cover as the commercial US single. Contains the edited version of *Cornflake Girl* from the US single as well as the LP version.

US Promo CD Single (Front)

US Promo CD Single (Insert)

US Promo CD Single (Back)

US Promo CD Single (Disc)

God (US)

CD Single
Atlantic PRCD5398-2
January 1994

1 God (3:55)

Atlantic released the US *God* promotional-only CD single in three different versions. The first contains only the 3:55 LP version of *God* and includes the lyrics on the back of the insert. All three versions were packaged in jewel boxes with the cover being a cropped and brighter version of the UK *Cornflake Girl* part one CD single.

US 1-Track Promo CD Single (Front)

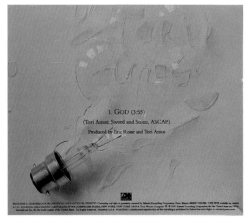

US 1-Track Promo CD Single (Back)

US CD (Disc)

God (US)

CD Single
Atlantic PRCD5408-2
January 1994

1 God (LP Version 3:55)
2 Home On The Range (5:25)
3 The Waitress (LP Version 3:07)

The second version of the *God* promotional-only CD single contains two additional tracks, *Home On The Range*, and the LP version of *The Waitress*. This version features white printing on the cover, unlike the other two versions which feature name and title printed in black. *Home On The Range* was mistakenly not identified on the CD as being the Cherokee Edition.

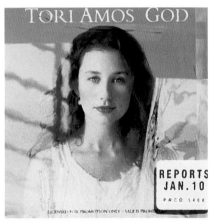

US 3-Track Promo CD Single (Front)

US 3-Track Promo CD Single (Back)

God (US)

CD Single
Atlantic PRCD5573
March 1994

1 God (No Guitar 3:58)
2 God (Some Guitar 3:58)
3 God (LP Version 3:58)

Some radio stations thought that the original version of *God* was a little too heavy on reverb so Atlantic issued this promotional-only radio-friendly version which allowed you to decide how much guitar you wanted *God* to contain. This version also includes the lyrics to *God* and a silver disc, unlike the previous two versions in which the discs were white. This version is the hardest to find of the three *God* promotional-only CDs.

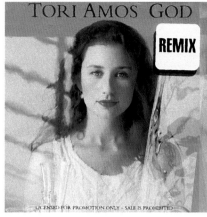

US 3-Track Promo Remix CD Single (Front)

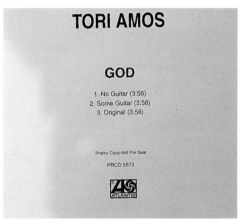

US 3-Track Promo Remix CD Single (Back)

US 3-Track Promo Remix CD Single (Disc)

US 3-Track Promo CD Single (Disc)

God (UK)

12" Single
East West SAM1418 (August 1994)

1 God (The Thinking Mix 2 10:00)
2 God (Acapella Vocal and Rain
   Mix 4:42)
3 God (The Rainforest Resort
   Mix 10:40)
4 God (The CJ Bolland Mix 5:54)

4-track promotional-only 12" in black stickered
sleeve. Contains the same tracks as the
commercial *God* 12" release. The 4-track "mixes"
promotional-only cassette includes the same
tracks as the CD single while the 6-track
promotional-only cassette includes tracks from
the CD single and the 12" single.

UK Promo Remix Cassette

UK Promo 6-track Cassette

God (UK)

12" Single
East West SAM1424
August 1994

1 God (Dharma Kaya Mix 12:34)

1-side UK promotional-only 12" in black
stickered sleeve. Features the *Dharma
Kaya Mix* by The Joy from the *God* UK CD
single.

UK Promo 1-Sided 12" Single

UK Promo 12" Single (A-Side)

UK Promo 12" Single (B-Side)

Little Drummer Boy (Australia)

CD Single
East West LDB 1
1994

    1 Little Drummer Boy (3:20)

Very rare Australian 1-track promotional-only CD single released from the *Under The Pink* Australian and New Zealand 2-CD Tour Edition.

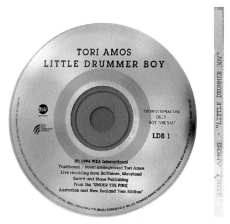

Australian Promo CD Single
(Disc and Spine)

Past The Mission (US)

CD
Atlantic PRCD5815-2
1994

    1 Past The Mission (4:05)
    2 Winter (Live 6:37)
    3 The Waitress (Live 3:29)
    4 Icicle (Live 7:50)
    5 Past The Mission (Live 4:21)
    6 PSA 1 (:30)
    7 PSA 2 (:60)

Seven-track promotional-only CD includes four live tracks taken from the two UK *Past The Mission* CD singles and two short public service announcements from Tori regarding R.A.I.N.N. One of the hardest-to-find US promotional singles.

US Promo 7-Track CD Single (Front)

US Promo 7-Track CD Single (Back)

Past The Mission (US)

CD Single
Atlantic PRCD 5888
1994

    1 Past The Mission (4:05)

US Atlantic 1-track radio promotional-only CD single comprising of a silver disc with no insert; name and title on CD and inlay-card only.

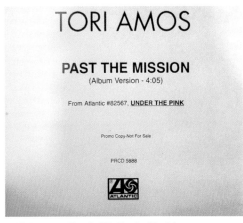

US Promo 1-Track CD Single (Back)

US Promo 1-Track CD Single (Disc)

Past The Mission (UK)

CD Single
East West SAM 1361
1994

    1 Past The Mission (4:05)

UK 1-track promotional-only CD single of *Past The Mission*, features a positive photographic image on the disc, unlike the commercial UK version which has a reverse image. The German *Past The Mission* CD single and the Australian CD single also have the positive image disc.

UK Promo CD Single (Insert)

UK Promo CD Single (Disc)

Tea With The Waitress (US)

CD
Atlantic PRCD5498-2
March 1994

Promotional-only interview CD with
Washington D.C.'s Bob Waugh from
WHFS FM. Part one features the complete
interview with Tori (25:52) and selected
bits from *Under The Pink*. Part two has
Tori giving the answers only (14:12) so
any local DJ could appear to conduct his
or her own interview (the questions and
introductions to the answers are provided
on the insert).

Advance CD-R (Front)

Boys For Pele (US)

CD
Advance CD-R of
Boys For Pele
(1995)

Recordable CD sent
out at the end of
November. Only a few
of these CD-Rs are
known to exist making
them virtually
unobtainable.

Tea With The Waitress (Front)

Advance CD-R (Back)

Tea With The Waitress (Back)

Tea With The Waitress (Disc)

Advance CD-R (Disc)

New Music From Tori Amos (US/Germany)

US Promo CD (Front)

CD
(*US*) Atlantic PRCD6535-2
December 1995
(*Germany*) WEA International PRCD 128

1 Cornflake Girl (5:05)
2 God (3:57)
3 Silent All These Years (4:10)
4 Crucify (Remix 4:58)
5 These Precious Things (sic) (4:25)
6 China (4:58)
7 Me And A Gun (3:43)
8 Past The Mission (4:04)
9 Smells Like Teen Spirit (3:15)

US Promo CD (Back)

Nine-track promotional-only sampler with a somewhat misleading title. The cover reads "New music from Tori Amos…." Upon opening the jewel box reveals the rest of the title to be "…is coming soon." The cover features a beautiful shot of a reposing Tori, complete with temporary tattoo on her right arm. The cover also features a sticker "Look For Tori's new single in stores January 2nd 1996!"

The track listing mistakenly titles *Precious Things*, "*These Precious Things*" and also incorrectly lists *Crucify* as the remixed version. The German version contains the same tracks. It only differs in catalog number and that the US CD is silver complete with track listing while the German version is a black CD with Tori's name only.

US Promo CD (Disc)

German Promo CD (Disc)

Holiday Greetings (US)

CD
Atlantic PRCD6589
December 1995

In December 1995 Atlantic issued a brief (46-second) promotional-only CD intended for radio with six different holiday messages from Tori. Although there are six messages contained on the CD, greetings two and six as well as one and five are identical in their content. They only differ slightly in their delivery. Tori sounds rather restrained on all but one of the greetings. The CD itself is a plain silver disc in a jewel box with the heading "Tori Amos Holiday Greetings" and the track listing. There is no insert, just Tori's name, the title, track listing, catalog number, "promotional" line and Atlantic logo on the reverse of the jewel case.

Greeting 1
"Hi, this is Tori Amos, wishing happy New Year and a Merry Christmas."

Greeting 2:
"Hey there, this is Tori Amos wishing everybody a happy holiday and a happy New Year."

Greeting 3:
"Hi there, this is Tori Amos wishing everybody a happy holiday."

Greeting 4:
"Hi, this is Tori Amos, wishing everybody happy New Year."

Greeting 5:
"Hi, this is Tori Amos wishing happy new year and a Merry Christmas."

Greeting 6:
"Hey there, this is Tori Amos wishing everybody a happy holiday and a happy New Year."

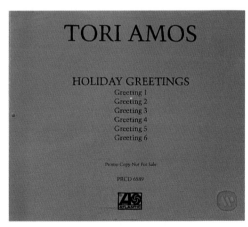

US Promo CD (Back)

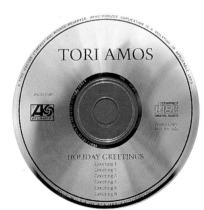

US Promo CD (Disc)

Boys For Pele (US)

Cassette EP
Atlantic PRCS 6608
December 1995

1 Caught a Lite Sneeze (Edit 3:59)
2 Hey Jupiter (5:10)
3 Talula (4:08)
4 Putting The Damage On (5:08)

Prior to the full length album's advance cassette release, Atlantic issued a 4-track promotional-only sampler cassette. The cover, a beautiful shot of Tori is actually a cropped version of the shot from the CD insert of Tori suckling a pig. This was the first time that the edited version of *Caught A Lite Sneeze* appeared. It would later resurface on the *Caught A Lite Sneeze* US promotional-only CD single.

Cassette
Atlantic 82862-4
January 1996

The advance promotional full-length cassette release for *Boys For Pele* featured only a white J-card with the track listing and title printed in black. No rare cover art this time.

There were no advance promotional CD or vinyl copies of *Boys For Pele* until just days before the actual street date of January 23rd, 1996, when commercial copies with gold Atlantic promotional stamps were sent out. However, in early December 1995 several CD-R (recordable CD) discs were sent out from the studio to a few intimate friends and associates.

US Advance 4-Track Sampler Promo Cassette   US Advance Full Length Promo Cassette

Boys For Pele (UK)

UK Advance Cassette (Front) UK Advance Cassette (Back)

Cassette
East West
December 1995

East West UK *Boys For Pele* full-length advance promotional cassette. The cover denotes on the front and back that the tape is a promotional copy. Track listing remained the same as the commercial version.

Cassette Sampler #1
East West

    1 Talula (4:08)
    2 Caught A Lite Sneeze (4:24)
    3 Father Lucifer (3:43)
    4 Professional Widow (4:31)
    5 Mr. Zebra (1:07)
    6 Hey Jupiter (5:10)
    7 Putting The Damage On (5:08)

UK East West promotional-only sampler cassette issued prior to *Boys For Pele*.

Cassette Sampler #2
East West

    1 Talula (4:08)
    2 Caught A Lite Sneeze (4:24)
    3 Putting The Damage On (5:08)
    4 Father Lucifer (3:43)
    5 Mr. Zebra (1:07)
    6 Hey Jupiter (5:10)

The second UK East West promotional-only cassette sampler for *Boys For Pele*. This version, unlike the earlier advance cassette, comes with a four-color cover, the track sequence is slightly different and *Professional Widow* has been omitted from this version. The cover shot reverses the photo from the *Caught A Lite Sneeze* CD singles.

UK Cassette Sampler #1 (Front and Spine)

UK Cassette Sampler #2 (Front) UK Cassette Sampler #2 (Back and Spine)

Boys For Pele (Germany)

CD
East West PROP100
December 1995

German advance CD for *Boys For Pele* comes in a slim jewel-case with the release date (1.19.96) noted on the cover.

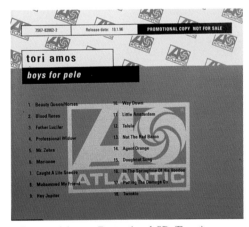

German Advance Promotional CD (Front)

German Advance Promotional CD (Disc)

Caught A Lite Sneeze (US)

CD Single
Atlantic PRCD 6549-2
January 1996

> 1 Caught A Lite Sneeze (Edit 3:59)
> 2 Caught A Lite Sneeze (LP Version 4:24)

US 2-track promotional-only CD single features the edited version of *Caught A Lite Sneeze*, which was not found on the US commercial release.

US Promo CD Single (Front)

US Promo CD Single (Disc)

Caught A Lite Sneeze (US)

Cassette Single
Atlantic PRCS 6574
January 1996

Atlantic promotional-only cassette of *Caught A Lite Sneeze* featured the edited version (3:59) of the track, repeated three times on each side of the cassette. White J-card with black printing "*Caught A Lite Sneeze (Edit)*."

US Promo Cassette (Front)

Caught A Lite Sneeze (Australia)

CD Single
East West TA-3
January 1996

    1 Caught A Lite Sneeze (3:59)
    2 Talula (4:08)
    3 Muhammad My Friend (3:48)

Beautiful promotional-only sampler from Australia features two album tracks and the edited version of *Caught A Lite Sneeze*. Packaged in a slim jewel case with no cover artwork. This is the only time that *Muhammad My Friend* has appeared on a single.

Australian Promo CD Sampler

Caught A Lite Sneeze (UK)

CD Single
East West A5524CDDJ
January 1996

    1 Caught A Lite Sneeze (Radio Edit 4:00)

UK promotional 1-track picture CD of *Caught A Lite Sneeze* (*Radio Edit* 4:00).

UK Promo CD Single (Front)

UK Promo CD Single (Back)

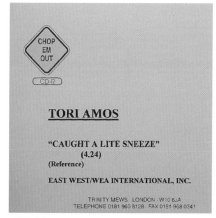

UK Advance Promo CD-R (Front)

UK Promo CD Single (Disc)

UK Advance Promo CD-R (Disc)

London Girls (France)

CD Single
East West/FNAC PROC 95368
February 1996

1 London Girls (3:20)
2 That's What I Like Mick
  (The Sandwich Song) (2:59)
3 Samurai (3:03)

Unique French promotional-only CD single was actually given away free with the purchase of *Boys For Pele* in France for a limited time. Packaged in a cardboard sleeve, a few managed to find their way into the UK and US.

French Promo CD Single (Front)

French Promo CD Single (Back)

Talula (UK)

CD Single

East West A8512CDDJ
March 1996

1 Talula (The Tornado Mix 3:43)
2 Talula (LP Version 4:21)

12" Single
East West SAM 1797

1 Talula (BT's Synethasia Mix 11:27)
2 Talula (The Tornado Mix 3:43)

Cassette Single (6-Track)

1 Talula (The Tornado Mix 3:43)
2 Talula (BT's Synethasia Mix 11:27)
3 Amazing Grace/Til' The Chicken (6:48)
4 Frog On My Toe (3:40)
5 Sister Named Desire (5:29)
6 Alamo (5:11)

Cassette Single (1-Track)

1 Talula (The Tornado Mix 3:43)

The UK *Talula* promotional-only CD single takes the *Tornado Mix* from the UK CD singles while the distinctive and very rare promotional-only 12" includes two tracks from the UK part two CD single. This unique 12" was the only version of *Talula* to be released on vinyl anywhere. The 6-track cassette contains all the tracks from the two UK CD singles.

French Promo CD Single (Disc)

TORI AMOS

"TALULA"
(Tornado mix)
3.43

WEA International.

UK CD-R (Front)

UK CD-R (Disc)

UK Cassette Promo
6-Track)

UK 12" Promo Single (Front)

UK Promo CD Single (Front)

UK Cassette Promo
(1-Track)

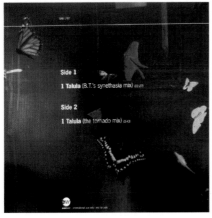

UK 12" Promo Single (Back)

UK Promo CD Single (Disc)

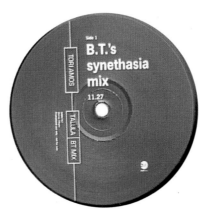

UK 12" Promo Single (A-Side)

UK 12" Promo Single (B-Side)

Talula (US)

CD Single
Atlantic PRCD 6720
May 1996
Radio Version

1 Talula (The Tornado Mix Edit 3:43)
2 Talula (Tornado Album Version 3:43)
3 Samurai (3:03)
4 Frog On My Toe (3:40)
5 London Girls (3:20)
6 Talula (BT's Synethasia Mix 11:27)

US Radio Promo (Front)

US Radio Promo (Back)

US Radio Promo (Disc)

Talula (US)

CD Single
Atlantic PRCD6736-2
May 1996
Retail Version

1 Talula (The Tornado Mix 3:22)
2 Talula (Tornado Album Version 3:45)
3 Samurai (3:03)
4 Frog On My Toe (3:37)
5 London Girls (3:20)
6 Talula (BT's Synethasia Mix 11:27)

Atlantic released two different versions of the *Talula* promotional-only single, the first intended for radio and the second for retail in-store play. They contain the same tracks although the radio version has the timings of several tracks printed incorrectly on the insert and disc. These promotional-only CDs were almost the same as the US commercial release of *Talula*, the only difference being that the promotional versions added *Talula* (*The Tornado Mix* 3:32).

US Promo CD Single (Disc)

US Promo CD Single (Front)

US Promo CD Single (Back)

Professional Widow (US)

12" Single
Atlantic DMD2305
June 1996

1. Professional Widow
   (Armand's Star Trunk Funkin'
   Mix 8:08)
2. Professional Widow
   (Just Da Funk Dub 3:44)
3. Professional Widow
   (MK Mix 7:20)
4. Professional Widow
   (MK Vampire Dub 6:56)

US white sleeve promotional 12" includes the same tracks as the commercial version released the following month. Unlike the commercial release, the promotional copy features an original red and black Atlantic label. This was the version that was shipped to clubs leading to Tori's second number one single in Billboard. Ironically, during *Professional Widow*'s two-week stay at number one on the Billboard "Dance/Club Play" chart, *Boys For Pele* dropped out of the Billboard Top 200 album chart for the first time since its release.

US Promo 12" (Front)

US Promo 12" (A-Side)

US Promo 12" (B-Side)

Hey Jupiter (US)

CD Single
Atlantic PRCD 6801
July 1996

1. Hey Jupiter (Dakota Version)
   (Edit 4:05)
2. Hey Jupiter (Dakota Version)
   (Long 6:03)
3. Hey Jupiter (Album Version 5:10)

First and harder to find of the two US *Hey Jupiter* promotional-only CD singles includes both the radio edit from the UK 12" single and the long version from the UK and US CD singles. This version comes in a jewel box with no cover, just the track listing printed on the back of the CD and a silver and red Atlantic label.

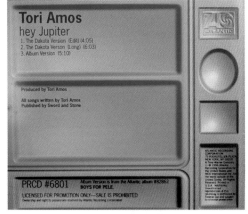

US Promo CD Single #1 (Back)

US Promo CD Single #1 (Disc)

Hey Jupiter (US)

CD Single
Atlantic PRCD6812-2
July 1996

1 Hey Jupiter (Dakota Version)
(Edit 4:05)
2 Hey Jupiter (Dakota Version)
(Long 6:03)
3 Hey Jupiter (Album Version 5:10)

The second and more common US *Hey Jupiter* promotional-only CD single contains the same tracks as the earlier version. The packaging is different in that it is essentially the same as the commercial US CD single; the principal difference, apart from the catalog numbers, being that the commercial release is a digipak while the promotional version comes in a jewel box. The disc, like the commercial UK and US singles, is a picture CD, although dull and unintelligible compared to the UK and US commercial CDs.

US Promo CD Single #2 (Front)

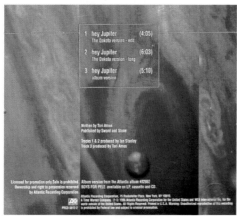
US Promo CD Single #2 (Back)

US Promo CD Single #2 (Disc)

Hey Jupiter/ Professional Widow (UK)

CD Single
East West A5494CDDJ
July 1996

1 Hey Jupiter (Dakota Version) (Edit 4:05)
2 Professional Widow (Armand's Star Trunk Funkin' Mix) (Edit 3:45)

UK promotional-only single takes two tracks from the commercial UK *Hey Jupiter/Professional Widow* singles, *Hey Jupiter (Dakota Version)* (*Edit* 4:05) from the 12" single and *Professional Widow (Armand's Star Trunk Funkin' Mix)* (*Edit* 3:45) from the CD single. The advance CD-R includes the long version of *Hey Jupiter*, which was later to be found on the commercial UK CD single.

UK Promo CD Single (Front)

UK Promo CD Single (Disc)

Professional Widow (UK)

12" Single
East West SAM 1867
August 1996

1 Professional Widow (Armand's Star Trunk Funkin' Mix 8:08)
2 Professional Widow (Just Da Funk Dub 3:44)

Scarce UK 12" promotional-only release, includes two tracks from the US commercial 12" release and comes packaged in a unique picture sleeve with a completely different cover from any other version of *Professional Widow*.

TORI AMOS

"HEY JUPITER"
(Dakota version, 6:03)
"PROFESSIONAL WIDOW"
(Armand's Star Trunk Funkin' Mix
Radio Edit, 3:45)

For: EAST WEST.

WEA INTERNATIONAL INC.

UK Promo CD-R (Front)

UK Promo CD-R (Disc)

UK Promo 12" Single (Front)

UK Promo 12" Single (Back)

UK Promo 12" Single (A-Side)

UK Promo 12" Single (B-Side)

In The Springtime Of His Voodoo (US)

12" Single
Atlantic DMD2320
August 1996

1 In The Springtime Of His Voodoo
   (Hasbrouck Heights Club Mix 10:00)
2 In The Springtime Of His Voodoo
   (Quiet Mix 4:24)
3 In The Springtime Of His Voodoo
   (Sugar Dub 8:53)
4 In The Springtime Of His Voodoo
   (Hasbrouck Heights Single Mix 4:22)

Like the US *Professional Widow* promotional 12",
this promotional 12" includes the same tracks as
the commercial version released the following
month. The black and white Atlantic label is
virtually identical to the commercial version with
the exception of the catalog numbers and
promotional markings. Atlantic had hoped to
repeat the dance club success that *Professional
Widow* enjoyed; unfortunately *In The Springtime
Of His Voodoo* peaked at number six.

Atlantic's Back To School Survival Kit (US)

CD
Atlantic PRCD 6385
1995

18-track Atlantic
promotional-only CD
features the unlikely
inclusion of *A Case Of
You*. This CD is exactly
the same as the *Spew
U* compilation released
earlier in the fall of
1995.

ATLANTIC'S BACK TO SCHOOL SURVIVAL KIT

1. CIV "So Far, So Good...So What" (2:11)
2. MACHINES OF LOVING GRACE "Richest Junkie Still Alive" (4:02)
3. DRAGMULES "Send Away" (4:12)
4. THE INBREDS "Any Sense Of Time" (3:42)
5. THE CHARLATANS "Just Lookin'" (3:48)
6. SMILE "Staring At The Sun" (3:42)
7. JILL SOBULE "Supermodel" (3:11)
8. RUSTY "Misogyny" (5:34)
9. 7 MARY 3 "Cumbersome" (3:45)
10. FRANCIS DUNNERY "Too Much Saturn" (3:57)
11. SUGAR RAY "10 Seconds Down" (Live Version) (4:14)
12. SUPERNOVA "Math" (2:16)
13. THE HATTERS "Colors" (4:12)
14. EDWIN McCAIN "Solitude" (4:33)
15. JUNIOR BROWN "Sugarfoot Rag" (2:40)
16. B-TRIBE (featuring Deborah Blando) "Nanita" (4:17)
17. TORI AMOS "A Case Of You" (4:38) (previously unreleased)
18. JEWEL "Angel Standing By" (2:38)

Promo Copy-Not For Sale
PRCD 6385

US Promo CD

US Promo 12" (Front)

US Promo 12" (A-Side)

US Promo 12" (B-Side)

Check It Out (US)

CD
WEA WEA CIO-92
1992

18-track WEA (Warner-Elektra-Atlantic) compilation includes LP version of *Crucify*.

US Promo Sampler CD (Front)

US Promo Sampler CD (Back)

Encomium: A Tribute To Led Zeppelin Sampler (US)

CD
Atlantic PRCD 6117-2
April 1995

4-track Atlantic promotional-only CD single for the Led Zeppelin tribute CD includes the Tori/Robert Plant duet *Down By The Seaside* (7:49).

US Promo CD Sampler

Go!-Go! (Japan)

CD
Atlantic ASCD-69
March 1994
Atlantic ASCD-71
May 1994
Atlantic ASCD-117
March 1996

Japanese East West/Atlantic promotional-only compilation CDs. The March 1994 CD includes *Cornflake Girl* and *God*, May 1994 includes *Pretty Good Year* and March 1996 includes *Caught A Lite Sneeze*.

Go!-Go!: March 1994

Go!-Go!: May 1994

Hit Disc (US)

CD
TM Century 023B
December 1993

18-track promotional-only CD issued to radio for broadcast on December 17th, 1993. Although broadcast just prior to Christmas, Tori performs the only Christmas song on the CD, *Little Drummer Boy*.

Hit Disc: Radio Show CD

Go!-Go!: March 1996

I'm On Fire (US)

CDS
Atlantic PRCD6858-2
October 1996

1 I'm On Fire (3:07)

The first single from the excellent *VH-1 Crossroads* CD is Tori's live version of Bruce Springsteen's *I'm On Fire*. The promotional-only single, unlike the full-length CD, does not contain the video for *I'm On Fire*.

US Promo CD Single

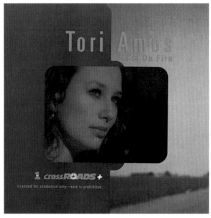

US Promo CD Single (Front)

J. Spew (US)

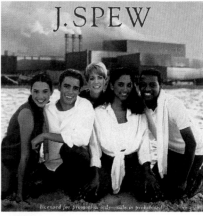

CD
Atlantic PRCD 6599-2
1996

17-track Atlantic promotional-only sampler includes *Caught A Lite Sneeze* (*Edit* 4:00) and *Mr. Zebra*. The packaging is an amusing take-off on J. Crew catalogs featuring color selections such as radioactive waste / smog / decay / sludge / muck and pond scum.

US Promo Sampler (Front)

US Promo Sampler (Back)

In Concert (US)

2-CD
Westwood One 93-94
August 1993

1 Crucify
2 Silent All These Years
3 Happy Phantom
4 Girl
5 Whole Lotta Love
6 Leather
7 Smells Like Teen Spirit
8 China

Radio Show produced and distributed by The Westwood One Radio Network for broadcast the week of August 16th, 1993. The show consists of two parts: CD1 is Pearl Jam and CD2 is Tori. These discs are very rare as only a few hundred were produced. Recorded 9.4.92 at The Coach House, San Juan Capistrano, CA USA.

Westwood One: In Concert, 1993

Tom Jones: I Wanna Get Back With You (US)

CD Single
Atlantic PRCD 6047

Atlantic promotional-only CD single includes title track duet with Tori

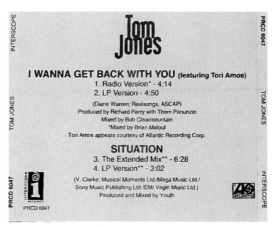

US Promo CD Single

97

Music For The Rest Of Us (US)

CD
Atlantic PRCD 5695-2

14-track Atlantic promotional-only sampler includes *Past The Mission*.

Promo CD Sampler #1

Music For The Rest Of Us (US)

CD
Atlantic PRCD 4763-2

10-track Atlantic promotional-only CD includes *Crucify* and *Precious Things*.

Promo CD Sampler #2

Modern Rock Live (US)

CD
Friday Morning Quarterback FMQBMR32
March 1994

16-track promotional-only radio show features a live version of *Icicle*.

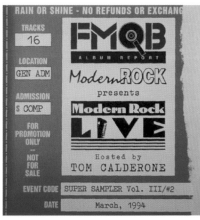

CD Front

Music For The Rest Of Us (US)

CD
Atlantic PRCD 4787

10-track Atlantic promotional-only CD includes *Crucify* and *Precious Things*.

Promo CD Sampler #3 (Front)

Music For The Rest Of Us

Everything But The Girl · "Alison" (3:04)
Clannad · "Harry's Game" (2:30)
Máire Brennan · "Beating Heart" (4:12)
Tori Amos · "Crucify" (4:58)
Enya · "The Celts" (2:56)
Everything But The Girl · "Tougher Than The Rest" (4:13)
Clannad · "In A Lifetime" (Duet with Bono) (2:08)
Máire Brennan · "Jealous Heart" (4:36)
Tori Amos · "Precious Things" (4:26)
Enya · "To Go Beyond (II)" (2:58)

Promo Copy-No: For Sale

PRCD 4737

ATLANTIC

Promo CD Sampler #3 (Back)

On The Edge (US)

CD
Westwood One 94-13
March 1994

1 Crucify
2 Cornflake Girl
3 Pretty Good Year
4 Silent All These Years
5 God

Westwood One radio CD intended for broadcast the weekend of March 26th, 1994. The CD is split between Tori and Sarah McLachlan.

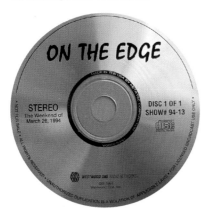

On The Edge 1994 (Cue-Sheet)

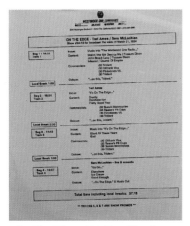

On The Edge 1994 (Disc)

Pro Mo (Brazil)

CD
WEA CDP0994
1994

13-track Brazilian Warner-Elektra-Atlantic promotional-only sampler CD includes the album version of *Cornflake Girl* (5:05).

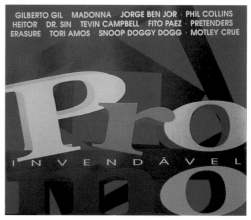

Brazillian CD Sampler

Spew 5 (US)

CD
Atlantic PRCD5564-2

18-track Atlantic promotional-only sampler includes *Cornflake Girl*.

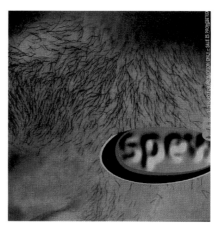

US Promo CD Sampler

US Promo CD (Front)

US Promo CD (Back)

So This Is Christmas (US)

CD
Atlantic PRCD 5996
1994

1 Bad Religion—Silent Night
2 Hootie & The Blowfish—The Christmas Song
3 Daniel Johnson—Rudolph The Red-Nosed Reindeer
4 Victoria Williams—Have Yourself A Merry Little Christmas
5 Collective Soul—Blue Christmas
6 Tori Amos—Little Drummer Boy
7 Evan Dando—Silent Night
8 Juliana Hatfield—Make It Home

Atlantic released two promotional-only Christmas samplers of Atlantic artists performing mostly traditional Christmas songs in 1994, the first being *So This Is Christmas* and then later, *You Sleigh Me*. Tori appeared on both, performing *Little Drummer Boy*, which would not be released commercially until it appeared next on the Australian Limited Edition double CD of *Under The Pink and More Pink*. The two CDs are slightly different: Tori, Hootie and The Blowfish, Victoria Williams, and Juliana Hatfield appear on both CDs while Bad Religion, Daniel Johnson, Collective Soul and Evan Dando appear only on *So This Is Christmas*.

Spew U (US)

CD
Atlantic PRCD 6360-2
1995

18-track Atlantic promotional-only sampler includes *A Case Of You*. Same tracks as Atlantic's *Back To School Survival Kit*.

US Promo CD Sampler (Front)

US Promo CD Sampler (Back)

Spin This (US)

CD

18-track Spin Magazine CD sampler includes *Crucify*.

US Promo Sampler

Warner Music United Kingdom (UK)

CD
WEA PROMO CD 60
1994

WEA UK in-store-play promotional-only CD includes *Cornflake Girl* as both the opening and closing tracks.

Promo Sampler CD

You Sleigh Me (US)

CD
Atlantic PRCD5995
1994

1 Hootie & The Blowfish—The Christmas Song
2 Mary Karlzen—Run Run Rudolph
3 Billy Pilgrim—Let It Snow
4 Victoria Williams—Have Yourself A Merry Little Christmas
5 Melissa Ferrick—White Christmas
6 Tori Amos—Little Drummer Boy
7 Everything But The Girl—25th December
8 Jill Sobule—Xmas Song
9 Juliana Hatfield—Make It Home

Contains tracks from *So This Is Christmas*, as well as exclusive to this CD, Mary Karlzen, Billy Pilgrim, Melisa Ferrick, Jill Sobule and Everything But The Girl.

US Promo CD

Miscellaneous Promotional Items

Cornflake Girl (US)

Promo Cereal Box

Atlantic US issued a real Kellogg's Corn Flakes box with a sticker simply reading "Tori Amos… Cornflake Girl." The lot number on the top of the box is 04074NC. At some point, there were counterfeits produced whereby someone reproduced the stickers and applied them to boxes. The original sticker is very clear and semi-gloss. There is also a UK version of the box; however, on the UK version, the colors are darker, muddled and less vibrant than the US version. The box was a very limited item. If you should find one for sale, make sure you verify the authenticity of the box.

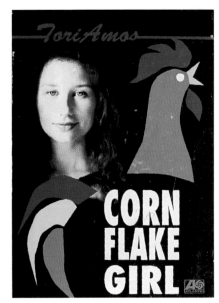

Cornflake Girl Promotional Cereal Box

Boys For Pele (UK)

Photo Book

East West UK issued a limited 36-page 5" x 6" color and black and white photo book that includes a total of 50 photos, the majority of which are out-takes or previously unseen shots. There are no credits or text but most of, if not all, the shots are from Cindy Palmano. The book has a bright orange cover with 'Tori Amos' in the upper left hand corner. The book itself comes in a slip-case, also bright orange and also with Tori's name in the same spot. These were extremely scarce when the album first came out and seemed to get easier to procure as time went on. Some did make their way to the US where Atlantic distributed them as promotional items.

UK Promotional Photo Book (Sleeve)

UK Promotional Photo Book (Centerfold)

Entertainment Weekly (US)

Atlantic Promo Magazine
1992

Atlantic took every press clipping and review they could find—a substantial number by this time—and compiled them in their entirety, photos and all, into this 22-page magazine with a take-off of an Entertainment Weekly cover. The reviews are primarily from the UK and include raves from Q, Elle, New Musical Express, Time Out, Melody Maker, Vox and many more. Atlantic then used it promote Tori to music retail and radio in the US.

Atlantic Promo Magazine (Front)

Atlantic Promo Magazine (Back)

Little Earthquakes (US)

Atlantic Promo Hat
1992

Very limited and rarely seen Atlantic promotional hat given away as a promotional item during the summer 1992 US *Little Earthquakes* tour. Extremely hard to find.

US Promo Hat

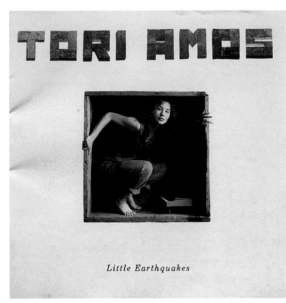

Little Earthquakes Promo Book

Little Earthquakes (US)

Atlantic Gold Record Award

Gold Record award presented to Tom Richards at Upside Down in 1992 in recognition of sales of 500,000 copies of *Little Earthquakes*.

Little Earthquakes Gold Record Award

Little Earthquakes (US)

US Promo Oversize Lyric Book

Beautiful 40-page oversize (9.125" X 9.25") lyric book with color cover and black and white photos inside. Eight of the 12 tracks are accompanied by a velum page with a line from each song printed in red ink.

Crucify
I've been looking for a savior in these dirty sheets
I've been looking for a savior beneath these dirty sheets

Silent All These Years
sometimes I hear my voice and it's been here silent all these years

Precious Things
my loyalties turned like my ankle in the seventh grade running after Billy running after the rain

Happy Phantom
they say Confucius does his crossword with a pen

China
in your eyes I saw a future together…you just look away in the distance

Mother
we told you all our secrets all but one

Tear In Your Hand
maybe she's just pieces of me you've never seen

Little Earthquakes
give me life give me pain give me myself again
here we go again these Little Earthquakes

Need A Drink? (US)

Listening Party Invitation

Boys For Pele "Need A Drink?" Atlantic listening party invitation sent out to press, record retailers and distributors in various cities around the US in January and February 1996.

Need A Drink? Party Invitation

Royal Albert Hall: Party Invitation

East West invitation to an after show party with Tori after the March 8th, 1996 show at London's Royal Albert Hall. There were about 200 people present and Tori was presented with a gold record award for *Boys For Pele*.

Party Invitation

Sounds Like Tori Amos! (US)

US Promo Deodorant Stick

Atlantic Records, bought "Teen Spirit" deodorant packages and applied a bright orange sticker reading "Sounds Like Tori Amos!" There were far fewer of these than the later "Cornflake Girl" cereal box which was equally bizarre.

Sounds Like Tori Amos
Promotional Deodorant
Stick

The Tori Story: Promotional Publication

The Tori Story!: Tori Amos On Tour (US)

US Promo Publication

Atlantic issued this 20-page compilation of US and Canadian press clippings revolving around the short promotional tour Tori performed in April and May of 1992 before embarking on the full blown *Little Earthquakes* tour the following month. Very well done and very hard to find.

Japanese Pre-Release Advert

Under The Pink (Japan)

Japanese Pre-release Ad

Japanese pre-release advert includes the photo that was to have been the original cover for *Under The Pink*. This particular sheet was signed by Tori.

Winter Promo Sno Dome

Winter (US)

Sno Dome

Atlantic US promotional-only plastic snow dome released in 1992 to tie in with the release of the *Winter* CD single. Very scarce promotional item.

Under The Pink Platinum Record Award

Under The Pink (US)

Atlantic Platinum Record Award

Atlantic Records Platinum Record award presented to Tom Richards at Upside Down in 1994 in recognition of more than 1 million copies sold of *Under The Pink*.

Under The Pink Magazine Reprint

Under The Pink (US)

US Promo Magazine Reprint

Atlantic promotional reprint of Billboard magazine article from Dec 4th, 1993.

US Promo Poster

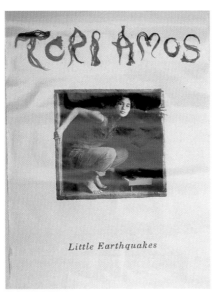

US Promo Poster

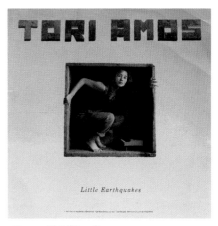

Promo Flat (Front)

Promo Flat (Back)

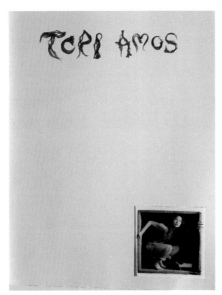

US Promo Biography (Front)

US Promo Biography (Opened)

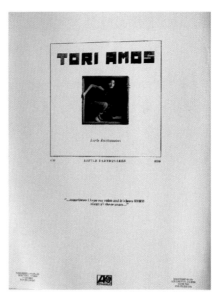

US Promo Biography (Back)

TORI AMOS
Little Earthquakes

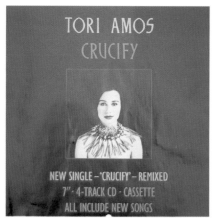

US Promo Card

French Promo Counter Display
(Reads "Sultry on the Airwaves")

UK Promo Counter Display

UK Promo Flat

UK Promo Counter Display

US Promo CD Bin Divider

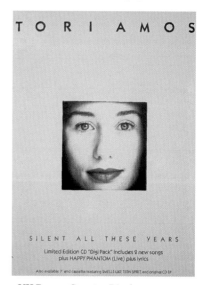

US Promo Poster

UK Promo Counter Display

US Promo Flat (Front)

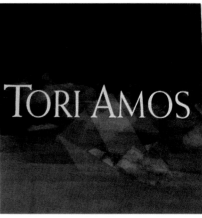

US Promo Flat (Back)

US Poster

Atlantic Promo Biography (Front)

US Promo Poster

US Promo Poster

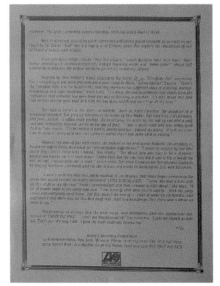

Atlantic Promo Biography (Back)

Atlantic Promo Postcard

US Promo CD Bin
Divider Card

German Ad

UK Promo Biography (Front)

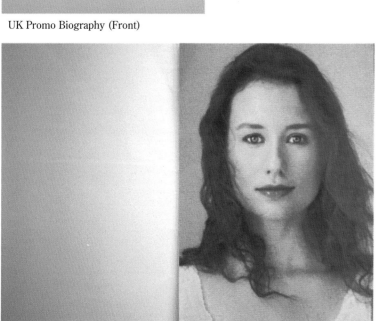

UK Promo Biography (Inside)

UK Promo Counter Display

27" x 30" UK Promo Standup

US Promo Poster

UK Promo Counter Display

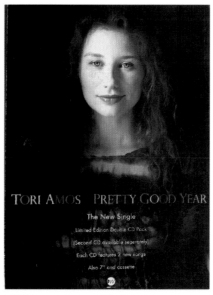

UK Promo Counter Display

US Promo Poster

Magazine Covers: US Promo Poster

US Promo Flat (Front)

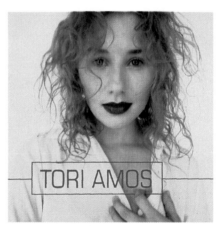

US Promo Flat (Back #1)

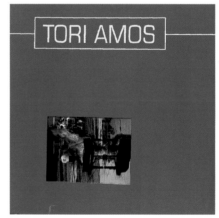

US Promo Flat (Back #2)

US Promotional Sweatshirt

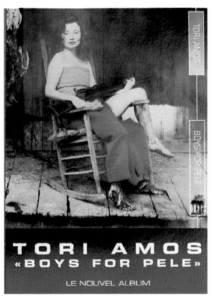

French Promo Postcard

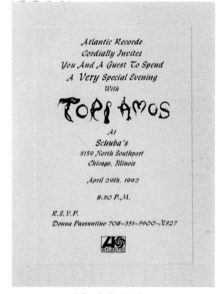

Atlantic Invitation:
Schuba's April 29th, 1992 Chicago

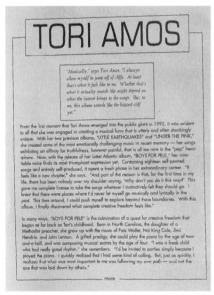

27" x 30" UK Promo Standup

UK Promo Counter Display

US Promo Biography

Royal Albert Hall: Backstage Passess March 8th And 9th, 1996

Blender
Volume 2.2 (US)

CD-ROM Magazine

US CD-ROM magazine includes a Tori feature entitled "Ten Fingers And A Cheap Keyboard." This includes four short video interviews with Tori ranging from 45 seconds to almost two minutes. It also includes a US album discography and a partial list of Tori web sites. The interfaces are beautifully done while *Agent Orange* plays in the background.

Boys For Pele
(UK)

Box Set
UFO TORI 2

UK 12" x 12" box set put out by UFO Music Ltd. This is an aftermarket item and not an official piece. The box contains the UK *Boys For Pele* CD (although some boxes were made available without the CD), the *Cornflake Girl* book by Susan Wilson and a 8.25" x 11.75" color print of Tori.

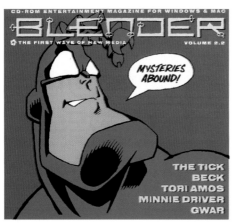

Blender v2.2: CD-ROM

UK Box (Front)

UK Box (Back)

Boys For Pele
(US)

Wooden Box
1996

Very nicely crafted 6" x 6" wooden box with a laser-etched drawing of Tori on the top. Apparently made by the same company that put out the *Little Earthquakes* laser-etched wooden box. Includes the US *Boys For Pele* CD. This box is limited to 1000 copies and therefore easier to find than the *Little Earthquakes* box which was limited to 250 copies.

Laser-Etched Wooden Box (Top)

Laser-Etched Wooden Box (Open)

Flexi-Discs (Russia)

Two flexi-discs came out of Russia in 1994: *Space Dog* and *God.* Each came in a paper sleeve and each was issued in three different colors. The sound quality is poor, the sleeves look like they were made on a office copier but they are unique and a unusual addition to any Tori collection.

Space Dog Russian Flexi-Disc (Sleeve)

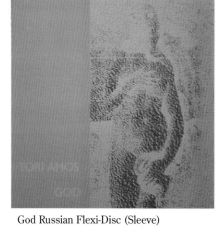

God Russian Flexi-Disc (Sleeve)

Space Dog Russian Flexi-Disc (Clear)

God Russian Flexi-Disc (Clear)

Space Dog Russian Flexi-Disc (Yellow)

God Russian Flexi-Disc (Green)

Space Dog Russian Flexi-Disc (Blue)

God Russian Flexi-Disc (Blue)

Kim Fowley: Let The Madness In (US)

CD
Receiver Records RRCD203
1995

The enigmatic Kim Fowley had originally entitled his 1995 album "*Tori Amos Songbook and Other Delights*" and planned to include cover versions of *Leather* and *Past The Mission*. The title was changed to "*Let The Madness In*" and the cover versions were dropped from the album after Kim was unsuccessful in obtaining permission to cover those tracks. The album does however include Kim's peculiar tribute to Tori called "*Tori Amos Drinking Teardrops In The Twilight Zone*" and a remix of that track called "*Tori Amos Part 2.*"

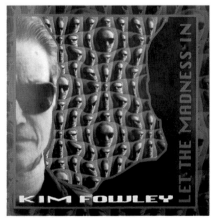

US CD (Front)

Hey Jupiter (UK)

Box Set
UFO
July 1996

8" x 8" aftermarket box made to hold the *Hey Jupiter* CD Single. Includes a 36-page color and black and white photo book with some previously unseen photos and also, a beautiful 7" x 7" color glossy shot of Tori. Brought to you by UFO, the same people who made the *Pink Earthquakes* and *Boys For Pele* box sets. Limited to 2000 copies.

UFO Box (Front)   UFO Box (Back)

Jawbox: Jawbox (US)

CD
Atlantic 92707-2
1996

Atlantic label-mates Jawbox cover *Cornflake Girl* on their 1996 self-titled album. The song is a hidden track that begins several minutes after the last track has ended and include slightly altered lyrics.

Interview CD and Book (UK)

Carlton Books/Sound & Media Ltd.
1996

Repackaging of the Mick St. Michael CD-sized book adding new artwork and an interview CD. There are four interviews included on the CD. The interviews are licensed from Westwood One and were recorded just prior to the release of *Boys For Pele*. The audio quality of the interviews is excellent and Tori even does bits of *American Pie* and *Caught A Lite Sneeze*. Although repackaged and released in late Summer 1996, the contents of the book have not been updated and don't touch on anything post *Under The Pink*.

CD and Book (Front)

CD and Book (Back)

Launch Issue #6 (US)

CD-ROM Magazine

CD-ROM magazine (May 1996) features Tori performing *Marianne* live in Los Angeles as well as an interview with Tori as a waitress/bartender proffering a menu of topics ranging from *Professional Widow* to explaining why she always thanks the Fairies on all her albums. ("Because I'd be stupid not to.")

Launch v6: CD-ROM

Little Earthquakes (US)

Wooden Box Set
1992

Wooden box with a laser-etched portrait of Tori on the top. The box includes the US *Little Earthquakes* CD and the UK *Silent All These Years* CD single. The box measures 10" x 5" x 1". Limited to only 250 copies, these are very hard to find. This is an unofficial piece and not to be confused with the French *Little Earthquakes* wooden box which was a sanctioned promotional item.

Laser-Etched Wooden Box (Top)

Laser-Etched Wooden Box (Open)

Marbury House (US)

Newspaper Ad

Original newspaper advertisement for Tori's 1983 Tuesday through Saturday appearances at The Lion's Gate Tavern in The Marbury House in Georgetown, MD USA. This copy of the ad is signed by Tori.

Advertisement For Tori Show 1983

Pink Earthquakes (UK)

BOX SET
UFO
1994

Aftermarket UK 12" x 12" box contains the UK *Under The Pink* CD, four color postcards, a 50-page color and black and white soft cover photo book called '*Pink Earthquakes*' and a 'Certificate Of Authenticity.' Whenever a piece of product comes with a 'Certificate Of Authenticity', beware, because it's a futile attempt to authenticate the product which is almost always an unofficial release.

UK UFO Box (Front)

UK UFO Box (Back)

Postcard Singles (Poland)

A very bizarre version of *Little Earthquakes* came out of Poland in 1992. The entire album, in the form of 12 cardboard postcard singles, was released. Upon close inspection, you can actually see the grooves pressed into the postcards. The sound quality leaves quite a lot to be desired; nevertheless they are an interesting addition to any collection.

Crucify: Polish Postcard Single (Front)

Crucify: Polish Postcard Single (Back)

Girl: Polish Postcard Single (Front)

Girl: Polish Postcard Single (Back)

Silent All These Years: Polish Postcard Single (Front)

Silent All These Years: Polish Postcard Single (Back)

Precious Things: Polish Postcard Single (Front)

Precious Things: Polish Postcard Single (Back)

Winter: Polish Postcard Single (Front)

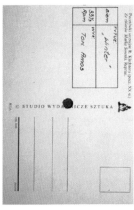

Winter: Polish Postcard Single (Back)

Happy Phantom: Polish Postcard Single (Front)

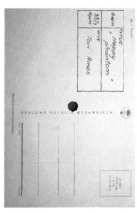

Happy Phantom: Polish Postcard Single (Back)

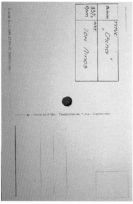

China: Polish Postcard
Single (Front)

China: Polish Postcard
Single (Back)

Leather: Polish Postcard
Single (Front)

Leather: Polish Postcard
Single (Back)

Mother: Polish Postcard
Single (Front)

Mother: Polish Postcard
Single (Back)

Tear In Your Hand: Polish
Postcard Single (Front)

Tear In Your Hand: Polish
Postcard Single (Back)

Me And A Gun: Polish
Postcard Single (Front)

Me And A Gun: Polish
Postcard Single (Back)

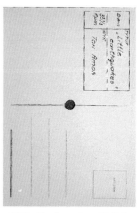

Little Earthquakes: Polish
Postcard Single (Front)

Little Earthquakes: Polish
Postcard Single (Back)

R.A.I.N.N (US)

Pamphlet/CD Single
Atlantic PRCD 6032

R.A.I.N.N., The Rape, Abuse and Incest National Network was set up with help from Tori, Atlantic Records and the Warner Music Group. It is a non-profit organization based in Washington, DC USA that operates a 24-hour national toll-free hotline (1.800.656.HOPE) for victims of sexual abuse. Tori wanted there to be a place for people to reach out to when they didn't know where else to go. For that reason R.A.I.N.N. was established. Ironically Tori is not found on the CD although it does include public service announcements by Michael Stipe, Mike Mills, Frente!'s Angie Hart and more.

Set List/ Times For Things

Set list and day's schedule for *Under The Pink* show at The Opera House—Seattle, WA USA September 14th, 1994.

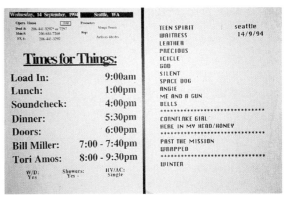

Under The Pink Tour: Sept. 19th, 1994

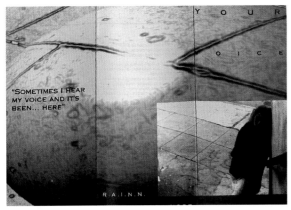

R.A.I.N.N. Pamphlet

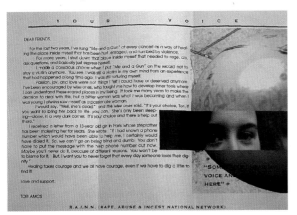

R.A.I.N.N. Pamphlet

R.A.I.N.N. Promo CD

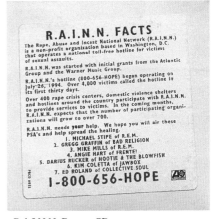

R.A.I.N.N. Promo CD

Tori's Top Ten

In the May 1994 issue of England's 'Vox' Magazine, Tori listed her ten favorite records.

1 Aretha Franklin
Amazing Grace

2 Led Zeppelin
The Box Set

3 The Doors
LA Woman

4 Nine Inch Nails
The Downward Spiral

5 Joni Mitchell
Blue

6 Miles Davis
Sketches Of Spain

7 Janis Joplin
Cheap Thrills

8 Patti Smith
Horses

9 Beatles
Revolver

10 Sex Pistols
Never Mind The Bullocks

Faye Wong: Faye Best (China)

CD
Cinepoly CP50129

Chinese superstar Faye Wong covers *Silent All These Years* on her 1994 greatest hits CD.

Faye Wong CD (Front)

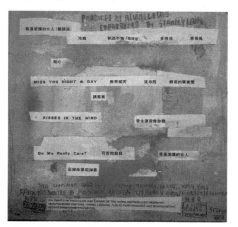

Faye Wong CD (Back)

five

chapter five
*collaborations
and guest works*

B.T.: Blue Skies (UK)

CD Single: Part 1
Perfecto PERF130CD1
October 1996

CD Single: Part 2
Perfecto PERF130CD2

12" Single
Perfecto PERF130T

Promotional 12" Single: Part 1
Perfecto SAM 1910

Promotional 12" Single: Part 2
Perfecto SAM 1918

New trance/dance club music from BT (Brian Transeau). BT was responsible for remixing *Talula* (*BT's Synethasia Mix*). Tori returns the favor here appearing prominently on BT's new single *Blue Skies*.

UK CD Single Part 1

UK CD Single Part 2

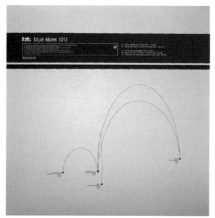

Part 1: UK Double Promo 12"

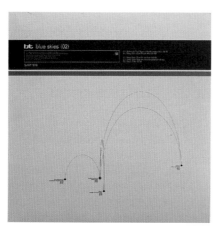

Part 2: UK Double Promo 12"

B.T.: Ima (US)

CD/2-CD
Perfecto/Reprise 46356-2
November 1996

Tori appears in the US on BT's 1996 album *Ima*. Tori is prominently featured on "*Blue Skies Featuring Tori Amos*"—according to the sleeve—and also on the 12:52 remix included on the album. The UK version of Ima is a single CD and does not contain *Blue Skies*. *Blue Skies* will appear on BT's forthcoming UK CD *ESCM*.

Sandra Bernhard: Without You I'm Nothing (US)

LP/CD/CS
Enigma 73369
1989

Tori sings background on *Little Red Corvette*.

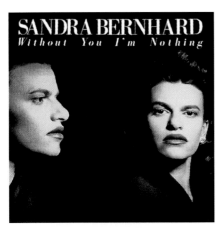

Without You I'm Nothing CD

Encomium: A Tribute To Led Zeppelin (US)

CD/CS
Atlantic 82731
April 1995

Tori duets with Robert Plant on *Down By The Seaside*, a track taken from Led Zeppelin's 1975 *Physical Graffiti* album.

Led Zeppelin Tribute CD

Cool Christmas: Various Artists (UK)

CD
Warner Music UK 9548-32485-2
October 1993

UK "Christmas" compilation stretches the title slightly with the inclusion of *Winter* instead of *Little Drummer Boy* as Tori's contribution, but the rest of the disc is pretty much on track. This excellent 18-track compilation also includes The Pogues, Pretenders, Enya, Aztec Camera, Tom Waits, Lou Reed, Chris Rea and more.

Cool Christmas CD

Escape From L.A.: Soundtrack (US)

CD/CS
Lava/Atlantic 92714
July 1996

Sequel to John Carpenter's *Escape From New York* includes the LP version of *Professional Widow* in the strange company of Gravity Kills, White Zombie, Ministry, Tool, Stabbing Westward, Butthole Surfers and more.

Escape From L.A.: Soundtrack CD

Eugina: Salt Tank (UK)

CDS
Internal ST6
1990

Rare UK CD Single by Eugina samples *Me And A Gun*.

Salt Tank CD Single

Ferron: Phantom Center (US)

CD/CS
Chameleon 74830
1990

Earthbeat
42576
1995 Reissue

Earthbeat
PRO-CD-7791
1995

Tori contributes background vocals to Canadian singer Ferron's 1990 album. The reissue has been remixed to highlight Tori's vocals with the exception of the first track, *Stand Up*, which mysteriously has been re-recorded, leaving Tori completely off the track.

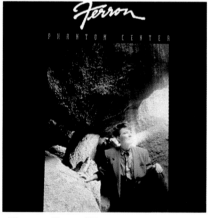
Phantom Center CD

Phantom Center Reissue CD

Higher Learning: Soundtrack (US)

CD/CS
Epic 66944
January 1995

Tori covers REM's *Losing My Religion* and performs her own beautiful new track *Butterfly*. This CD is the only place these two tracks can be heard. The lyrics and music to *Butterfly* can be found in the Bee Sides songbook.

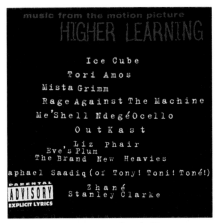

Higher Learning: Soundtrack CD

It Might Hurt A Bit: Unreleased Track

Tori and Michael Stipe duet, originally recorded for the soundtrack to *Don Juan Demarco* and then slated for release but left off of the *Empire Records* soundtrack. *It Might Hurt A Bit* has yet to see a release although Tori has promised to remix it and release it one day.

Phantom Center Promo CD Sampler

Tom Jones: The Lead And How To Swing It (US)

CD/CS
Atlantic 92457
October 1995

Includes *I Wanna Get Back With You*, a duet with Tori.

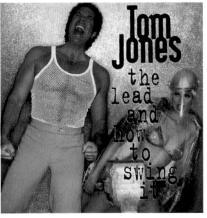

The Lead And How To Swing It CD

Tom Jones:
I Wanna Get Back With You (UK)

CD Single/7" Single/12" Single/
Cassette Single

Interscope 98796

I Wanna Get Back With You 7"

Kevin And Bean: We've Got Your Yule Logs Hangin' (US)

Cassette
KROQ KROQ CS-4
1993

Tori performs *Little Drummer Boy*. Alternative radio station KROQ in Pasadena, California put out this tape in 1992 with the proceeds going to charity. This was the first commercially available version of *Little Drummer Boy*. 10,000 of these were made and distributed only through Music Plus record stores in Southern California.

We've Got Your Yule
Logs Hangin' Cassette

Live At The World Café: Volume 1 (US)

CD
World Café WC9501
1995
Silent All These Years (*Live*)

WXPN FM, University of Pennsylvania's public radio station, released this CD as a benefit for public radio and it includes Tori performing *Silent All These Years* in the studio. Although the CD was released in 1995, the track was recorded much earlier.

Live At The World Café Volume 1: US CD

Mad @ Chris: This (UK)

12" Single
T:ME 0992
1992

Very rare UK double A Side promotional-only 12" samples *Me And A Gun*.

Mad @ Chris: This: UK Promo 7" Single

Stan Ridgway: Mosquitos (US)

LP/CD/CS
Geffen 24216
1989

Tori sings background vocals on three tracks: *Dogs*, *Peg* and *Pete And Me and The Last Honest Man*.

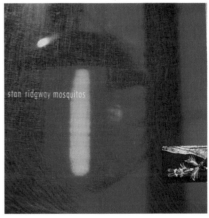

Stan Ridgway: Mosquitos CD

Rare On Air: Volume One (US)

CD
Mammouth MR0074-2
1994

In a wonderful coupling, *Rare On Air* has Leonard Cohen reading a short poem that segues into Tori performing a live, in-the-studio version of *Silent All These Years*. Recorded May 12th, 1992 at KCRW in Santa Monica, CA. This 15-track CD is a benefit for public radio and also includes John Cale, Natalie Merchant, Michael Penn, Nick Cave, Peter Himmelman, Evan Dando, Brendan Perry and others.

Rare On The Air Volume 1: US CD

Rolling Stone: Turn It Up (US)

MD
Rolling Stone RS-MD1
1994

16-track mini-disc compilation given away free to subscribers of Rolling Stone Magazine in the US in 1994. The album version of *Precious Things* is included as track number four.

Rolling Stone: Turn It Up Mini-Disc

Ruby Trax (UK)

3-LP/3-CD/2-CS
Forty Records NME40
1992

Forty-track compilation by some of 1992s alternative hitmakers performing their favorite number one hits from the previous forty years. This was released in the UK in celebration of New Musical Express' 40th anniversary with proceeds to benefit Cerebral Palsy. Tori covers *Ring My Bell*, a number one for Anita Ward in 1979. Other artists include Sinead O'Connor, Inspiral Carpets, Curve, Boy George, Bob Geldof, Suede, Jesus & Mary Chain, Blur, Aztec Camera, Billy Bragg and more. This compilation contains some wonderful tracks and is worth tracking down for more than just Tori's contribution.

Ruby Trax: CD

Ruby Trax: LP

Speaking of Christmas and Other
Things: US Cassette

Speaking Of Christmas and Other Things (US)

Cassette
KZON ZON101.5 FM
1992

Tori reads *Shel Silverstein's Sarah Sylvia Cynthia Stout Would Not Take The Garbage Out* with a somewhat sparse musical accompaniment dubbed in later, although not by Tori. Limited edition of 1000 only. Very difficult to find outside of KZON's market in Arizona.

Al Stewart:
Last Days Of The Century (US)

LP/CD/CS
Enigma 73316
1988

Tori sings background vocals on two tracks, *Red Toupee* and *Last Day Of The Century*, and plays piano throughout. Tori has also co-written a track on another Al Stewart album, *Famous Last Words*, called *Charlotte Corday*.

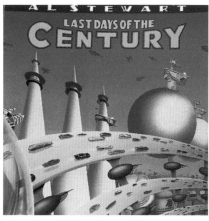
Last Days Of The Century CD

Famous Last Words CD

(Tess Makes Good)
China O'Brien:
Video (UK/US)

In 1988 a track called *Distant Storm* was used in the direct-to-video (except in Hong Kong!) martial arts film *China O'Brien*. *Distant Storm* is credited to Tess Makes Good but Ellen Amos is listed as contributing 'additional vocals'. The track is used only in the first few minutes of the film while China drives across the desert; it is relatively clean and free of dialogue. Although not written by Tori, the voice is unmistakable. When she heard the song years later, Tori remembered recording it but had had no idea it was ever used. Tori did however, remember being paid $150 to record it. It was recorded around the same time as *Y Kant Tori Read* and forgotten about. The film, by *Enter The Dragon* director Robert Clouse, stars Cynthia Rothrock as China, seeking revenge for her father's death at the hands of drug smugglers…etc. The video should be available for rental. Do not confuse this with the sequel several years later, *China O'Brien 2* which Tori does not appear on.

China O' Brien: UK Video

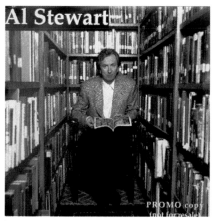
Famous Last Words Promo Sampler CD
(Front)

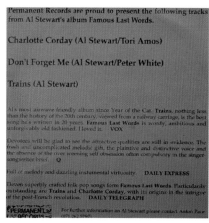
Famous Last Words Promo Sampler CD
(Back)

Toys: Soundtrack (US)

CD/CS
Geffen GEFD-24505
November 1992

Tori performs *The Happy Worker*. Tori was extremely unhappy with the final mix of this track, written and produced by Trevor Horn, and refused to allow a planned CD Single to be released.

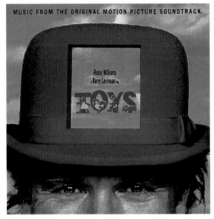

Toys: Soundtrack CD

Twister: Soundtrack (US)

CD/CS
Warner 46254
May 1996

Includes *Talula* (*BT's Tornado Mix*), the track that would replace the original version of *Talula* starting in late 1996 pressings of *Boys For Pele*.

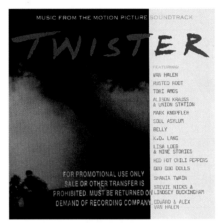

Twister: Soundtrack CD

Tower Of Song: Songs Of Leonard Cohen (US)

CD/CS
A&M 259-2
1995

Tribute CD includes Tori performing Cohen's *Famous Blue Raincoat*.

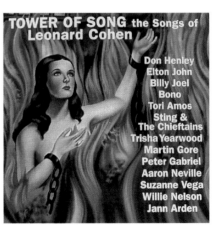

Tower Of Song CD

VH1's Crossroads (US)

CD/CS
Atlantic 82895
October 1996

Live compilation from the VH1 "Crossroads" series includes Tori performing Bruce Springsteen's *I'm On Fire* which was first broadcast June 19th, 1996. Tori also performed *Losing My Religion*, *Over The Rainbow* and *Sugar* during that session but only *I'm On Fire* appears here. Also included on the collection are Del Amitri, Gin Blossoms, Jewel, Blues Traveller, Melissa Etheridge with Joan Osborne, k.d. Lang, Chris Isaak, Goo Goo Dolls, Deep Blue Something, Edwin McCain, Son Volt and Pete Droge. The disc is an enhanced CD, playable on PCs or Macs, which features the video for *I'm On Fire* in addition to the audio track.

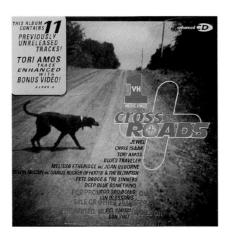
VH1's Crossroads CD

Virtuosity: Soundtrack (US)

CD
Radioactive RARD-11295
August 1995

Soundtrack includes the song *Party Man*, written by Tori and Peter Gabriel, although Tori does not appear on the track.

Virtuosity: Soundtrack CD

XSeSS Living Volume 3-1 (US)

CD-sized magazine including a 16-track CD that features Tori performing Leonard Cohen's *Famous Blue Raincoat* from the *Tower Of Song* CD.

XSeSS Living Volume 3-1 CD

You Sleigh Me (US)

CD
Atlantic 82851-2
November 1995

12-track Atlantic Christmas compilation includes Tori performing *Little Drummer Boy*. This was the first major label release of this track in America. This CD is a mixture of tracks taken from two Atlantic promotional-only CDs issued in late 1994, *So This Is Christmas* and *You Sleigh Me*. Several tracks on the promotional CDs did not make it to this official release, but Donna Lewis, Dillon Fence, and James Carter were added to this compilation. (*see Misc. Promotional Items*). Also included on this CD are Juliana Hatfield, Everything But The Girl, Victoria Williams, Collective Soul, Mary Karlzen, Billy Pilgrim, Daniel Johnson, Fence, and Jill Sobule.

You Sleigh Me CD

chapter six

*videos
and tv
appearances*

videos: *commercial*

Little Earthquakes

A*VISION 50335-3
Time 55:00
October 1992

1 Silent All These Years (Video)
2 Leather (Live)
3 Precious Things (Live)
4 Crucify (Video)
5 Me And A Gun (Live for MTV Asia)
6 Little Earthquakes (Live)
7 China (Video)
8 Happy Phantom (Live)
9 Here. in My Head (Live)
10 Winter (Video)
11 Song For Eric (Live)

videos: *promotional*

Caught A Lite Sneeze (US)

US Atlantic Promo Video

US Video (Front)

UK Video (Front)

Australian Video (Front)

Cornflake Girl (US)

Atlantic promotional video for the UK version (3:50) of *Cornflake Girl*, which was shot in LA. It is a very different video from the US version shot later. This version is primarily black and white and evokes images of *The Wizard Of Oz* with its surreal shots of Tori spinning through space dressed in a white sack-like dress with a piano tied to her foot, only to end up falling into a giant spider web.

US Atlantic Promo Video
(UK Version)

Cornflake Girl (US)

Atlantic promotional video for the US version (3:54) of *Cornflake Girl*, which is quite different from the UK version. Tori drives a pick-up truck through the desert, picks up a young stud hitchhiking and Tori and girlfriends proceed to simmer him in a pot seasoned with carrots.

US Atlantic Promo Video
(US Version)

God (US)

US Atlantic Promo Video

Hey Jupiter (US)

Hey Jupiter (*Dakota Version*)—shortened to 3:55—is used for the promo clip instead of the album version.

US Atlantic Promo Video

139

Past The Mission (US)

US Atlantic Promo Video

Pretty Good Year (US)

US Atlantic Promo Video

Saturday Night Live (US)

Atlantic promotional video of Tori performing *Caught A Lite Sneeze* and *Hey Jupiter* on Saturday Night Live, January 20th, 1996.

US Atlantic Promo Video

Silent All These Years (UK)

UK East West promotional video includes an edited video version of *Silent All These Years* as well as the album version.

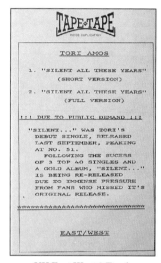

UK East West 2-Track
Promo Video

UK East West 2-Track
Promo Video

Silent All These Years (US)

Atlantic promotional-only video issued with at least three different variations. One version had only the *Silent All These Years* (4:16) video, the second version also added *Crucify* (*Live with band from The Jonathan Ross UK TV Show*) and *Crucify* (*Live with band from Late Night with David Letterman US TV Show*). The third version contained the live *Crucify* from the Jonathan Ross show, *Me And A Gun* (*Live from MTV Asia*), and *Silent All These Years* as the first and then repeated as the fourth and final track. *Silent All These Years* was voted number 98 of the Top 100 videos of all time by Rolling Stone magazine.

US Atlantic Promo Video

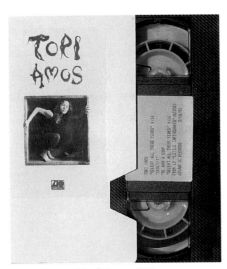

US Atlantic 4-Track Promo Video

Talula (US)

Talula (*The Tornado Mix*) is used for the video instead of the original album version. In late 1996, this version of *Talula* replaced the album version on all future pressings of *Boys For Pele*.

US Atlantic Promo Video

The Big Picture (US)

US Atlantic Promo Video

Tori Amos: Box Talk (US)

Cable TV interview with Tori prior to her appearance on *The Tonight Show with Jay Leno* February 12th, 1994.

US Atlantic Promo Video

Tori Amos: MTV Special (US)

Atlantic promotional-only video of MTV Special recorded March 4th, 1992 and first aired March 26th, 1992. This includes a running interview by MTV's John Norris cut with video clips of *Silent All These Years*, *China* and *Winter* as well as live performances of *Crucify*, *Me And A Gun* and *Precious Things*. Atlantic Records actually bid and won a charity auction for an hour of MTV air time and used the hour for this Tori special.

US Atlantic Promo Video

Under The Pink Video Compilation (Australia)

East West Australia

1 Cornflake Girl
2 God
3 Past The Mission
4 Pretty Good Year

Australian promotional-only video compilation of four *Under The Pink* tracks.

Video Compilation (Front)

Video Compilation (Back)

Tori Amos: Video Compilation (US)

1 Silent All These Years (4:16)
2 China (3:40)
3 Winter (4:38)
4 Crucify (4:22)
5 Smells Like Teen Spirit (Live 3:11)
6 God (3:54)
7 Cornflake Girl (3:54)
8 Pretty Good Year (3:38)
9 Past The Mission (4:19)
10 Caught A Lite Sneeze (4:25)

10-song Atlantic promotional-only video compilation. Released in very limited quantities in January 1996. This video includes all the promotional clips from the 1992 *Little Earthquakes* video compilation, omitting the live tracks, as well as *God, Cornflake Girl, Pretty Good Year* and *Past The Mission* from *Under The Pink*. The just-released *Caught A Lite Sneeze* from *Boys For Pele* and a live version of *Smells Like Teen Spirit*, recorded during the *Little Earthquakes* tour are also included.

US Atlantic Promo Video

tv appearances

1991

Jonathan Ross Show (UK)
11.22.91
Silent All These Years

Rapido (France)
12.11.91
Silent All These Years
Leather

1992

Wogan (UK)
1.29.92
China

MTV Special (US)
3.26.92
Silent All These Years
China
Winter
(Videos)
Crucify
Me And A Gun
Precious Things (Live)

People Today (UK)
3.30.92
(Videos)
Winter
Silent All These Years
China

Dini Petty Show
Me And A Gun
Crucify

David Letterman (US)
4.23.92
Crucify

Dennis Miller (US)
5.12.92
Silent All These Years
Crucify

Tonight Live (Australia)
5.22.92
Winter
Interview

Saturday At Rick's (Australia)
5.23.92
Interview

The Afternoon Show (Australia)
5.23.92
Winter (Video)
Interview

World Tonight (Australia)
5.25.92
Winter
Interview

The Midday Show (Australia)
5.27.92
Crucify
Interview

The Noise (Australia)
5.27.92
Leather
Silent All These Years (Video)

MTV Australia (Australia)
5.29.92
Interview
Winter (Video)

Good Morning Britain (UK)
6.19.92
Interview
Crucify (Video)

ABC In Concert (US)
6.20.92
Interviews
Me And A Gun
Silent All These Years
Crucify
Smells Like Teen Spirit

Summer Scene (UK)
6.24.92
Crucify
Interview

Top Of The Pops (UK)
6.25.92
Crucify

MTV Europe (UK)
8.10.92
Silent All These Years

Der Grosse Preiss (Germany)
8.20.92
Crucify

CBS This Morning (US)
9.9.92
Crucify
Silent All These Years (Video)

Arsenio Hall (US)
9.10.92
Silent All These Years

Night After Night (US)
10.31.92
Winter
Interview
Crucify (Video)

Tonight Live (Australia)
11.20.92
Silent All These Years
Interview

Elf 99 (Holland)
12.11.92
Crucify (Video)
Silent All These Years

1994

MTV Alternative Nation (US)
1994
Icicle

Top Of The Pops (UK)
1.20.94
Cornflake Girl

BBC TV "The Big E" (UK)
1.28.94
Interview

Today Show (US)
2.4.94
Baker Baker

Tonight Show (US)
2.12.94
God
Baker Baker

NBC's Friday Night (US)
2.19.94
Pretty Good Year

NBC's Friday Night (US)
3.12.94
Icicle

The Big Breakfast (UK)
3.16.94
Interview

David Letterman (US)
3.28.94
Cornflake Girl

Good Morning America (US)
3.30.94
Pretty Good Year

Top Of The Pops (UK)
3.17.94
Pretty Good Year

The Big Breakfast (UK)
3.23.94
Interview

TV5 (France)
4.20.94
Past The Mission
China

Jonathan Ross Show (UK)
5.1.94

Top Of The Pops (UK)
5.26.94

MTV (120 Minutes) (US)
6.20.94
Icicle

Conan O'Brien (US)
6.09.94
Cornflake Girl

David Letterman (US)
6.28.94
Precious Things

MTV (120 Minutes) (US)
7.4.94
Pretty Good Year

Tonight Show (US)
8.17.94

Morning News LA (US)
8.24.94
Pretty Good Year

Greg Kinnear (US)
8.25.94
Cloud On My Tongue

1993

Tonight Show (US)
1.12.93
Crucify
Winter

E! (US)
1.17.93
Winter
Interview
Crucify

1995

Tonight Show (US)
2.25.95
Butterfly

Later with Jools Holland
12.9.95
Interview

1996

ITV (UK)
1.3.96
Caught A Lite Sneeze

Top Of The Pops (UK)
1.11.96
Caught A Lite Sneeze

Saturday Night Live (US)
1.20.96
Caught A Lite Sneeze
Hey Jupiter

MTV (120 Minutes) (US)
1.21.96
Doughnut Song
Hey Jupiter
Muhammad, My Friend

Good Morning America (US)
1.26.96

MTV (120 Minutes) (US)
1.28.96
Horses

Today Show (US)
1.29.96

MuchMusic (Can)
1.29.96

CNN Showbiz Today (US)
1.30.96

Regis and Kathy Lee (US)
2.2.96
Putting The Damage On

Hotel Babylon (UK)
2.2.96
Hey Jupiter

CBS This Morning (US)
2.5.96
Doughnut Song

Tonight Show (US)
2.8.96

Musique Plus (Can)
2.13.96

MuchMusic (Can)
2.17.96

Friday Night Videos (US)
2.23.96
Caught A Lite Sneeze

Entertainment Tonight (US)
3.1.96

Nederland 3 (Hol)
3.11.96

The Big Breakfast (UK)
3.18.96

Heute Nacht (Ger)
3.19.96

Keynote (Ger)
3.19.96

Abendmagazin (Ger)
3.20.96

Harold Schmidt Show (Ger)
3.23.96

MTV "Hanging Out" (Ger)
4.1.96

VH-1 (Ger)
4.1.96

Pajama Party (UK)
4.6.96

David Letterman (US)
4.8.96

Kanal 4 Tapes (Ger)
4.27.96

Regis & Kathy Lee (US)
5.14.96

Conan O'Brien (US)
5.15.96
*In The Springtime Of His
Voodoo*

Today Show (US)
6.9.96

VH-1 Crossroads (US)
6.19.96
Losing My Religion
I'm On Fire
Over The Rainbow
Sugar

MTV Unplugged (US)
6.25.96

Tonight Show (US)
6.27.96
Hey Jupiter

Today In LA (US)
6.28.96
Mr. Zebra
Father Lucifer

E! (US)
7.1.96
Interview

Good Day LA (US)
7.16.96
Interview

MTV Unplugged (UK)
8.7.96 (UK Premiere)

Primetime Live (US)
8.21.96
Interview

David Letterman (US)
10.4.96
Father Lucifer

chapter seven
tori in print

Little Earthquakes (Songbook)

Amsco Publications AM 90041

Crucify / Girl / Silent All These Years / Precious Things / Winter / Happy Phantom / China / Leather / Mother / Tear In Your Hand / Me And A Gun / Little Earthquakes / Upside Down / Thoughts

MTV Unplugged (Songbook)

Amsco Publications AM 940258

Cornflake Girl / Blood Roses / Silent All These Years / Icicle / Caught A Lite Sneeze / Over The Rainbow / Hey Jupiter / In The Springtime Of His Voodoo

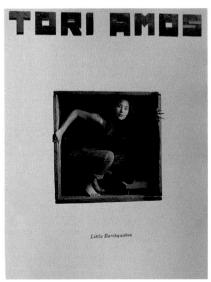

Little Earthquakes: Songbook (Front)

MTV Unplugged: Songbook (Front)

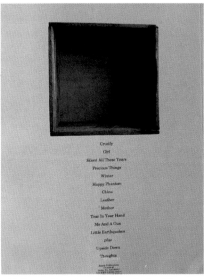

Little Earthquakes: Songbook (Back)

MTV Unplugged: Songbook (Back)

Under The Pink (Songbook)

Amsco Publications AM 92048

Pretty Good Year / God / Bells For Her / Past The Mission / Baker Baker / The Wrong Band / The Waitress / Cornflake Girl / Icicle / Cloud On My Tongue / Space Dog / Yes, Anastasia / All The Girls Hate Her / Over It

The Bee Sides (Songbook)

Amsco Publications AM 931315

Baltimore / Black Swan / Butterfly / Daisy Dead Petals / Etienne / Floating City / Flying Dutchman / Here. in My Head / Home On The Range (Cherokee Edition) / Honey / Humpty Dumpty / Mary / Ode To The Banana King (Part One) / Sister Janet / Song For Eric / Sugar / Sweet Dreams / Take To The Sky

Under The Pink: Songbook (Front)

The Bee Sides: Songbook (Front)

Under The Pink: Songbook (Back)

The Bee Sides: Songbook (Back)

Boys For Pele (Songbook)[†]

Amsco Publications AM 937750

Beauty Queen / Horses / Blood Roses / Father Lucifer / Professional Widow / Mr. Zebra / Marianne / Caught A Lite Sneeze / Muhammad My Friend / Hey Jupiter / Way Down / Little Amsterdam / Talula / Not The Red Baron / Agent Orange / Doughnut Song / In The Springtime Of His Voodoo / Putting The Damage On / Twinkle

Boys For Pele: Songbook (Front)

Boys For Pele: Songbook (Back)

All These Years (Biography)

Omnibus Press OP 47756
1994

Excellent and essential authorized biography by Kalen Rogers. 116 pages containing over 150 previously unseen photos, many From Tori's personal collection. *All These Years* is filled with fascinating biographical information beginning with Tori's childhood to covering the L.A. *Y Kant Tori Read* period to Tori's ascension to worldwide phenomenon. Includes discography and tour dates. Updated in late summer 1996 to include *Boys For Pele* information with 16 additional pages and over 30 new photographs as well as a beautiful new cover.

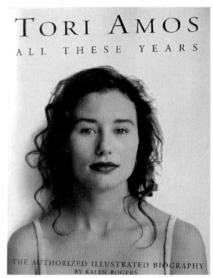

All These Years: Biography 1994

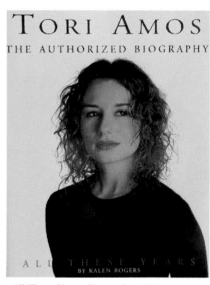

All These Years: Biography 1996

[†] *Worth noting: The original version of the* Boys For Pele Songbook *was banned by many libraries because of the controversial photo of Tori suckling a pig. Future editions will replace that photo with a politically correct shot.*

Under The Pink
(Tour Program)

Under The Pink
1994 Tour Program

Features an introduction by Neil Gaiman, author of the *Sandman* comic series. Neil, Tori's friend and confidant, is mentioned in *Space Dog*, *Horses* and *Tear In Your Hand*. Tour program also includes lyrics to *God*, *Cornflake Girl* and *Pretty Good Year* as well as photos taken during the recording of *Under The Pink*.

Boys For Pele
(Tour Program)

Boys For Pele
1996–97 Tour Program

Once again Neil Gaiman contributes a story, entitled "December 7th, 1995." The program includes many previously unseen photos as well as some beautiful paintings and the lyrics to *Doughnut Song*, *Horses*, *Mr. Zebra* and *Blood Roses*. Note that the tour program reads "1996–97", but the tour actually ended on November 11th, 1996.

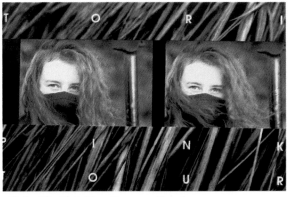

Under The Pink: Tour Program (Front)

Under The Pink: Tour Program (Back)

Boys For Pele: Tour Program (Front)

Boys For Pele: Tour Program (Back)

China (Sheet Music)

Winter (Sheet Music)

Winter: Sheet Music

China: Sheet Music

Cornflake Girl (UK)

1996 64-page color and b&w photo book with text by Susan Wilson. Also available packaged in the *Boys For Pele* aftermarket box set put out by UFO in the UK.

Cornflake Girl: Book

Death, The High Cost Of Living

By Neil Gaiman
DC Comics
November 1993

Introduction written by Tori for this compilation of Neil Gaiman's very popular *Sandman* comic series. Tori has also inspired a character in Sandman called Delirium in whom Neil has instilled some fairy-like traits such as scattering frogs and toadstools in her wake and coming up with ice cream flavors such as "Chicken and Telephone."

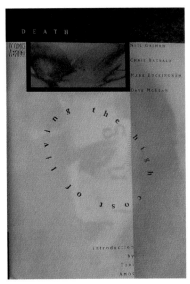
Death, The High Cost Of Living:
Book (Front)

Death, The High Cost Of Living:
Book (Tori Intro)

Pink Earthquakes

Book

Photo book that was included in the *Pink Earthquakes* UK box set.

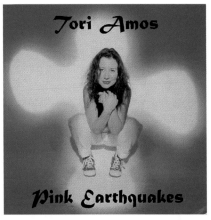
Pink Earthquakes: Book

Tori Amos

CD-sized book by Mick St. Michael is one of a series of books on major artists that includes photos, press clippings and stories generally culled from interviews and the music press. Repacked in 1996 together with an interview CD and a new cover.

Tori Amos: Book by Mick St. Michael

Women, Sex And Rock 'N' Roll

Fascinating 1995 paperback book by Liz Evans includes a lengthy interview with Tori as well as 13 other confessional stories by Bjork, Tanya Donnely, Kristen Hersch, Delores O'Riordan and other notable women musicians.

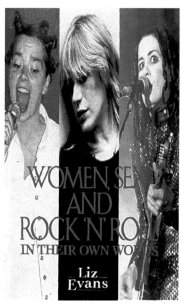

Women, Sex and Rock 'N' Roll: Book

Upside Down (Tori Amos Fan Club)

Tom Richards
PO Box 8456
Clearwater, FL 34618
USA
(FAX) 813.461.2922

Upside Down: Issue #1

Upside Down: Issue #3

Upside Down: Issue #2

Upside Down: Issue #4

Upside Down: Issue #5

Upside Down: Issue #6

Upside Down: Issue #7

Upside Down:
1996/1997 Calendar

Take To The Sky

UK Tori Amos Information Service

Steve Jenkins
25 Rydall Drive
Bexlyheath, Kent DA7 5EF
England

"Precious Things" was the original title of the UK magazine but later changed to "Take To The Sky" at Tori's request.

Take To The Sky:
Limited Re-issue of #1-2

Precious Things:
Issue #1

Take To The Sky:
Issue #2

Take To The Sky:
Issue #3

Take To The Sky:
Issue #4

Take To The Sky:
Issue #5

Take To The Sky:
Issue #9

Take To The Sky:
Issue #6

Take To The Sky:
Issue #7

Take To The Sky:
Issue #8

Really Deep Thoughts

Fanzine

Melissa and Richard Caldwell
PO Box 328606
Columbus, OH 48282
USA

Really Deep Thoughts:
Issue #1

Really Deep Thoughts:
Issue #2

Really Deep Thoughts:
Issue #3

Really Deep Thoughts:
Issue #4

Really Deep Thoughts:
Issue #5

magazine appearances

We have tried to include every major magazine appearance that Tori appears in, either as a complete article, photo(s) or a magazine review.

Not included here are the countless newspaper reviews and write-ups that have been appearing since 1980, as these would have been impossible to account for.

1988

Billboard
June 11, 1988

1991

What's On
October, 1991

Melody Maker
October 12, 1991

Melody Maker
September 14, 1991

New Musical Express
September 14, 1991

Melody Maker
November 16, 1991

International Musician
Christmas 1991

What's On In
Birmingham
December 21, 1991

1992

The ELLE Guide To
Living In Europe
January 1992

L.A. Rock
January 1992

Melody Maker
January 4, 1992

More
January 8-12, 1992

Billboard
January 11, 1992

New Musical Express
January 11, 1992

Time Out
January 22-29, 1992

New Musical Express
January 25, 1992

Entertainment Weekly
January 31, 1992

For Him Magazine
February 1992

HMV
February 1992

Keyboard Review
February 1992

New Woman
February 1992

Q (Cover)
February 1992

Q: February 1992

Q: 4-star Review
February 1992

Q: Little Earthquakes Ad
February 1992

Vox
February 1992

New Musical Express
February 8, 1992

Interview
March 1992

Billboard
March 7, 1992

New Musical Express
March 10, 1992

Billboard
March 11, 1992

Melody Maker
March 14/19, 1992

New Musical Express
March 21, 1992

Billboard
March 28, 1992

New Musical Express
March 28, 1992

HMV
April 1992

Vox
April 1992

Rolling Stone
April 2, 1992

Billboard
April 11, 1992

Rolling Stone
April 30, 1992

Creem
May 1992

Interview
May 1992

Musician
May 1992

Melody Maker
May 2, 1992

People
May 11, 1992

Stereo Review
June 1992

Vogue
June 1992

B Side
June/July, 1992

Glamour
August 1992

New Musical Express
August 15, 1992

Music Revue (Cover)
*August/September
1992*

Music Revue:
August 1992

Keyboard (Cover)
September 1992

Keyboard:
September 1992

VP/LS Preview
(Cover)
September 18, 1992

Network
*September/October
1992*

Rock Flash
October 1992

BAM - SF (Cover)
October 2, 1992

BAM - LA (Cover)
October 2, 1992

Bam:
October 1992

Spin
October 1992

Concert News
November 1992

Details
November 1992

Music Monitor (Cover)
November 1992

Philly Rock Guide
(Cover)
December 1992

Philly Rock Guide:
December 1992

Rolling Stone
December 10, 1992

1993

Musician
January 1993

Q
January 1993

Spin
January 1993

New Musical Express
February 6, 1993

B-Side
*February/March
1993*

Rolling Stone
March 4, 1993

Pulse
April 1993

Vox
April 1993

Keyboard
May 1993

Piano and Keyboard
(Cover)
May/June 1993

Goldmine
August 6, 1993

Rolling Stone
October 14, 1993

Q
November 1993

Billboard
December 4, 1993

1994

Schwann Catalog
(Cover)
1994

Schwann Catalog:
1994

New Review Of
Records (Cover)
*December/January
1994*

New Revue Of Records:
December/January 1994

Interview
January 1994

New Musical Express
January 1994

US
January 1994

Hits
January 17, 1994

Billboard
January 22, 1994

Calendar
January 30, 1994

Hits
January 24, 1994

Hits
January 31, 1994

Informant (Cover)
January 31, 1994

Impact
February 1994

Music Monitor
February 1994

Musician
February 1994

Performing Songwriter
February 1994

Q
February 1994

US
February 1994

Entertainment Weekly
February 4, 1994

Billboard
February 5, 1994

Hits
February 7, 1994

People
February 7, 1994

Hits
February 14, 1994

Entertainment Weekly
February 18-25, 1994

Billboard
February 19, 1994

Hits
February 21, 1994

Hot Press (Cover)
February 23, 1994

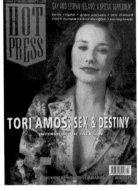

Hot Press:
February 23, 1994

Rolling Stone
February 24, 1994

Hits
February 28, 1994

Cosmopolitan
March 1994

Creem (Cover)
March 1994

Details
March 1994

Detour
March 1994

Creem:
March 1994

Bam:
March 11, 1994

Record Collector:
April, 1994

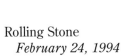

B Side:
April/May, 1994

Keyboard
March 1994

Mademoiselle
March 1994

Mojo
March 1994

Music Paper
March 1994

Q
March 1994

Slamm
March 1994

Spin
March 1994

Vox
March 1994

Hits
March 7, 1994

Bam - SF (Cover)
March 11, 1994

Bam - LA (Cover)
March 11, 1994

Hits
March 14, 1994

Melody Maker
March 19, 1994

New Musical Express
March 19, 1994

Hits
March 21, 1994

Hits
March 28, 1994

Informant
March 28, 1994

What's On
March 2-9, 1994

Spew
Spring 1994

Performing Songwriter
March/April 1994

Interview
April 1994

New Musical Express
April 1994

Record Collector
(Cover)
April 1994

Record Review
April 1994

Vox
April 1994

Hits
April 4, 1994

Hits
April 11, 1994

Informant
April 11, 1994

Hits
April 18, 1994

Christian Science
Monitor
April 22, 1994

Hits
April 25, 1994

New Musical Express
April 30, 1994

B Side (Cover)
April/May 1994

Island Ear
April/May 1994

NARM Sounding
Board (Cover)
April/May 1994

Music Monitor
May 1994

Q (Cover)
May 1994

Q:
May 1994

Vox (Cover)
May 1994

Vox:
May 1994

Hits
May 2, 1994

Rolling Stone
May 5, 1994

Hits
May 9, 1994

Hits
May 16, 1994

New Musical Express
May 21, 1994

Hits
May 23, 1994

Melody Maker
May 28, 1994

Hits
May 30, 1994

Audio
June 1994

Factor X
June 1994

Vogue
June 1994

Hits
June 6, 1994

Hits
June 13, 1994

Business Week
June 20, 1994

Hits
June 20, 1994

Rolling Stone
June 30, 1994

Music Monitor
July 1994

Select
July 1994

Beat
July 14, 1994

Jam (Cover)
July 22, 1994

Bone (Cover)
August 1994

Glamour
August 1994

Hits (Anniversary
Issue)
August 1994

Illinois Entertainer
(Cover)
August 1994

Interview
August 1994

Hits
August 1, 1994

Going Out (Cover)
August 5, 1994

Goldmine:
September 2, 1994

Illinois Entertainer:
August 1994

The Guide (Cover)
August 12, 1994

Billboard
August 13, 1994

L.A. Village View
August 19, 1994

Billboard
August 20, 1994

Music Monitor (Cover)
September 1994

Goldmine (Cover)
September 2, 1994

Rolling Stone
September 8, 1994

The Rocket
September 14, 1994

Billboard
September 17, 1994

Spin:
October, 1994

Keyboard:
November, 1994

Rolling Stone
September 22, 1994

The Guide
September 23, 1994

Billboard
September 24, 1994

Press Democrat
*September/October,
1994*

The Face
October 1994

Musician
October 1994

Spin (Cover)
October 1994

Rolling Stone
October 6, 1994

Keyboard (Cover)
November 1994

Rolling Stone
November 17, 1994

Playboy
November 1994

Billboard
December 7, 1994

Entertainment Weekly
December 9, 1994

New Musical Express
December 17, 1994

1995

Bone (Cover)
January 1995

Q
January 1995

Spin
January 1995

Rolling Stone
January 12, 1995

Rolling Stone
January 26, 1995

Details
February 1995

Rolling Stone
February 9, 1995

Shape
March 1995

Vox
March 1995

Musician (Cover)
April 1995

Select
May 1995

Veronica
May 13, 1995

B Side (Cover)
May/June 1995

Q
June 1995

Details
July 1995

Guitar
July 1995

Vox
July 1995

Music Week
December 11, 1995

New Musical Express
December 16, 1995

Time Out
December 20, 1995

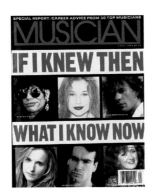

Musician:
April 1995

B Side:
May/June 1995

1996

Making Music
January, 1996

Next (Cover)
January 1996

Next:
January 1996

Q
January, 1996

Billboard
January 13, 1996

Rolling Stone
January 23, 1996

Q
February 1996

US
February 1996

People
February 5, 1996

Billboard
February 17, 1996

Newsweek
February 19, 1996

Diva
February/March 1996

Details
March 1996

Elle
March 1996

Musician
March 1996

Q
March 1996

React
March 1996

Seventeen
March 1996

Spin (Cover)
March 1996

Spin:
March 1996

Vox
March 1996

New Musical Express
March 30, 1996

Big O
April, 1996

George
April, 1996

Shift (Cover)
April 1996

Musician (Cover)
May 1996

Stereophile
May 1996

Vox
May 1996

People[†]
May 6, 1996

[†] *Tori named one of the 50 most beautiful people in the world.*

Time Out (NY)
(Cover)
May 8-15, 1996

B Side (Cover)
May/June 1996

Performance (Cover)
June 21, 1996

Rolling Stone
June 27, 1996

Billboard (Cover)
June 29, 1996

Details
July 1996

InStyle
July 1996

Entertainment Weekly
July 12, 1996

Brigitte
July 24, 1996

Shift:
April 1996

Musician:
May 1996

Time Out:
May 8-15, 1996

B-Side:
May/June 1996

The Face
October 1996

Q
October 1996

Mix
November 1996

Cosmopolitan
December 1996

Playboy
December 1996

Q
December 1996

US
December 1996

Spin
January 1997

chapter eight
bootlegs

8

e ig h t

Down Under The Pink '94

Red Robin ROB 1048A/B
Time 122:44
2-CD

CD 1: Tracks 1-15 recorded 12.10.94 at
The Festival Theatre, Adelaide,
Australia. CD 2: Tracks 1-4 6.7.92 Radio
JJJFM, Sydney, Australia. Track 5
recorded 11.26.94, Australian TV. Track
6 recorded 12.2.94 Radio JJJFM, Sydney,
Australia. Tracks 7-8 recorded 12.3.94,
Australian TV. Track 9 recorded 12.7.94,
Australian TV.

CD 1:
1 I'm On Fire
2 Crucify
3 The Waitress
4 Leather
5 Icicle
6 God
7 Honey
8 Precious Things
9 Me And A Gun
10 Angie
11 Cornflake Girl
12 Silent All These Years
13 American Pie
14 Smells Like Teen Spirit
15 Baker Baker

CD 2:
1 Precious Things
2 Crucify
3 Winter
4 Leather
5 Cornflake Girl
6 Interview
7 Interview
8 Cornflake Girl
9 Cornflake Girl

Down Under The Pink '94

Dreaming

Dreaming

Alley Kat AK046/47
Time 144:23
2-CD

CD 1 tracks 1-14 and CD 2 tracks 1-6
recorded 3.31.94 at The Sanders
Theater, Cambridge, MA USA.

CD 1:
1 Sugar
2 Crucify
3 Icicle
4 Precious Things
5 Happy Phantom
6 Pretty Good Year
7 God
8 Silent All These Years
9 The Waitress
10 Leather
11 Upside Down
12 Me And A Gun
13 Baker Baker
14 Cornflake Girl

CD 2:
1 A Case Of You
2 China
3 Past The Mission
4 Winter
5 Song For Eric
6 Cloud On My Tongue
7 Mother
   Amsterdam 4.7.94
8 Famous Blue Raincoat
   London 3.6.94
9 Ring My Bell
   Studio Outtake
10 Sarah Sylvia Cynthia Stout
   Live In Studio
11 Sweet Dreams
   Studio Outtake
12 The Happy Worker
   Studio Outtake
13 When I Was Dreaming
   Studio Outtake
14 China
   Chorale Arrangement, France 4.4.94
15 Love Song
   California 1994

Europe 1992

Rarities & Few RFCD 1314

Recorded 6.7.92 at
Alte Oper, Frankfurt, Germany.

1 New Shoes/Flying Dutchman
2 Crucify
3 Silent All These Years
4 Precious Things
5 Leather
6 Whole Lotta Love/Thank You
7 Upside Down
8 Happy Phantom
9 China
10 Tear In Your Hand
11 Me And A Gun
12 Winter
13 Smells Like Teen Spirit
14 Mother
15 Sugar

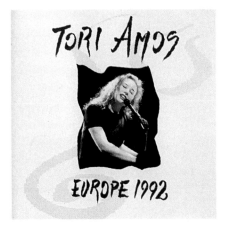

Europe 1992

Even More Rarities

Piano Classics PIC04

B-Sides and rarities.

1 A Case Of You
2 Honey
3 Black Swan
4 Home On The Range
5 Sister Janet
6 Daisy Dead Petals
7 Strange Fruit
8 All The Girls Hate Her
9 Over It
10 If 6 Was 9
11 Little Drummer Boy
12 Sarah Cynthia Sylvia Stout…
13 Ring My Bell
14 WHFS Interview
   (Tea With The Waitress)

Even More Rarities

Fairy Tales

Kiss The Stone KTS 353
Time 79:12

Tracks 1-11 recorded 4.29.94 at The Palladium, London, England. Tracks 12-15 recorded 7.29.94 at Raleigh Auditorium, Raleigh, NC USA

1 American Pie
2 Smells Like Teen Spirit
3 Icicle
4 Crucify
5 Happy Phantom
6 God
7 Silent All These Years
8 Bells For Her
9 Winter
10 Cornflake Girl
11 China
12 Leather
13 Upside Down
14 Cloud On My Tongue
15 A Case Of You

Fairy Tales

Forgotten Earthquakes

Amos 951
Time 78:08

Tracks 1-16 from CD Singles. Track 17 from Toys. Tracks 18-20 from *Little Earthquakes Demos and Outtakes* CD.

1 Upside Down
2 Thoughts
3 Sugar
4 Flying Dutchman
5 Humpty Dumpty
6 The Pool
7 Take To The Sky
8 Sweet Dreams
9 Crucify
10 Angie
11 Smells Like Teen Spirit
12 Thank You
13 Here. in My Head
14 Mary
15 Song For Eric
16 Ode To The Banana King
   (Part One)
17 The Happy Worker
18 Leather (Solo Piano Version)
19 Sarah Sylvia Cynthia Stout…
20 China (Solo Piano Version)

Forgotten Earthquakes

The Gipsy

Last Bootleg Records LBR015

Recorded 9.4/5.92 at
The Coach House, San Juan Capistrano,
CA USA.

1 Crucify
2 Silent All These Years
3 Happy Phantom
4 Girl
5 Whole Lotta Love
6 Leather
7 Smells Like Teen Spirit
8 China

The Gipsy

Goddess

Hurricane HURR041
Time 54:46

Tracks 1-4 recorded 2.5.96 at WDRE FM, New York, NY USA. Tracks 5-11 recorded 2.5.96 at WNEW FM, New York, NY USA. Tracks 12-13 recorded 1.6.96. Track 14 recorded 4.24.92 from David Letterman. Track 15 recorded 3.28.94 from David Letterman. Track 16 recorded 1994 at MTV studios.

1 Hey Jupiter
2 Thunder Road
3 Doughnut Song
4 Gary's Girl
5 Thoughts Of Mary Anne
6 Muhammad My Friend
7 Blood Roses
8 Unreleased Song
9 Sugar
10 Not The Red Baron
11 Caught A Lite Sneeze
12 Putting The Damage On
13 Hey Jupiter
14 Crucify
15 Cornflake Girl
16 Icicle

Goddess

I Like Led Zeppelin And I Love The Stones

Sugarcane Records SC52017/18
Time 129:26

CD 1 tracks 1-4 recorded 3.3.93 at WKQX-FM, Chicago, IL USA. Tracks 5-10 recorded 7.92 at Mountain Stage, Charleston, SC USA. CD 1 is the same as *Legend Of A Girl Child* CD. CD 2 recorded 11.8.92 at Page Hall, Albany NY. CD 2 is the same as *Thank You Angie* CD.

CD 1:
1 Crucify
2 Leather
3 Silent All These Years
4 Winter
5 Crucify
6 Silent All These Years
7 Happy Phantom
8 Me And A Gun
9 Winter
10 Smells Like Teen Spirit

CD 2:
1 Crucify
2 Silent All These Years
3 Precious Things
4 Happy Phantom
5 Leather
6 Tear In Your Hand
7 Whole Lotta Love
8 Thank You
9 Me And A Gun
10 Winter
11 Smells Like Teen Spirit
12 China
13 Angie

I Like Led Zeppelin and I Love The Stones

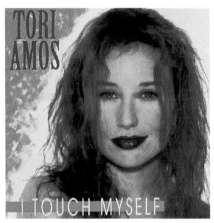
I Touch Myself

I Love Toffee Apples

Moas Music 001
Time 78:24

Recorded 5.2.94 at Civic Hall, Wolverhampton, England.

1 Crucify
2 Icicle
3 Precious Things
4 Leather
5 God
6 Silent All These Years
7 The Waitress
8 Honey
9 Bells For Her
10 Me And A Gun
11 Cornflake Girl
12 Here. in My Head
13 The Wrong Band
14 Sister Janet
15 A Case Of You

I Touch Myself

American Fly AF007
Time 79:20

Recorded 10.16.94 at Wharton Center, East Lansing, MI USA.

1 With A Little Help From My Friends
2 Yes, Anastasia
3 Leather
4 Icicle
5 The Waitress
6 God
7 Precious Things
8 Past The Mission
9 Bells For Her
10 Me And A Gun
11 Landslide
12 Cornflake Girl
13 China
14 I'm On Fire
15 Winter

I Love Toffee Apples

173

I'm On Fire

Kiss The Stone KTS 003A/B
Time 132:33
2-CD

CD 1 tracks 1-10, CD 2 tracks 1-5 recorded 10.26.94 at Palace Theater, New Haven, CT USA. CD 2 tracks 6-19 recorded 3.18.94 at World Café Interview.

CD 1:
1 I'm On Fire
2 Yes, Anastasia
3 The Waitress
4 Icicle
5 Leather
6 God
7 Precious Things
8 Honey
9 Bells For Her
10 Me And A Gun

CD 2:
1 Winter
2 Space Dog
3 Landslide
4 Past The Mission
5 Purple Rain
6 Intro
7 Precious Things
8 Interview
9 Pretty Good Year
10 Interview
11 Icicle
12 Interview
13 God
14 Interview
15 Cloud On My Tongue
16 Interview
17 Past The Mission
18 Interview
19 Baker Baker

I'm On Fire

In The Breeze

Blizzard BLZD141
Time 64:56

Tracks 1-5 recorded 2.1.96 from WXRT FM, Chicago, IL USA.Tracks 6-8 recorded 2.9.96 from KSCA FM, Los Angeles, CA USA. Tracks 9-10 recorded 2.11.96 from WHFS FM, Washington, DC USA. Tracks 11-12 recorded 2.96.96 at KEWD FM, Seattle, WA USA. Track 13 recorded 10.13.92 from the Alan Havey Show. Tracks 14-15 recorded 1994 from Friday Night Videos.

1 Little Amsterdam
2 Here. in My Head
3 Doughnut Song
4 Caught A Lite Sneeze
5 Putting The Damage On
6 Doughnut Song
7 Leather
8 This Old Man
9 Little Amsterdam
10 Thoughts Of Mary Ann
11 Crucify
12 Blood Roses
13 Winter
14 Pretty Good Year
15 Icicle

A Kiss On The Glass

Bullseye Records CD-EYE-22
Time 73:30

Recorded 5.6.92 at Backstage Tavern, Ballard, WA USA. The first Tori Amos bootleg.

1 Little Earthquakes
2 Crucify
3 Silent All These Years
4 Precious Things
5 Happy Phantom
6 Leather
7 Whole Lotta Love/Thank You
8 Upside Down
9 Me And A Gun
10 Winter
11 Smells Like Teen Spirit
12 Mother
13 China

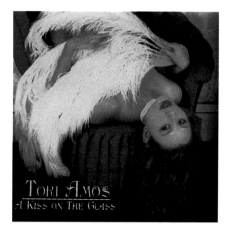
A Kiss On The Glass

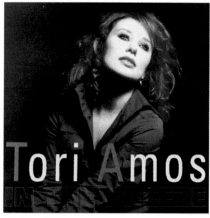
In The Breeze

L'Affaire d'Amoreuse

Montana MO10005
Time 67:43

Recorded 1993 from Radio Broadcast, Toronto, Canada. Same as *The Piano* And *On Tour*.

1 Smells Like Teen Spirit
2 Happy Phantom
3 Crucify
4 Silent All These Years
5 Precious Things
6 Leather
7 Tear In Your Hand
8 Whole Lotta Love
9 Little Earthquakes
10 Angie
11 Me And A Gun
12 China
13 Mother

L'Affaire d'Amoreuse

Last Temptation Of Tori

Alley Kat AK 051
Time 75:26

Recorded from Radio Broadcast, Berlin, Germany 4.9.94.

1 American Pie
2 Smells Like Teen Spirit
3 Pretty Good Year
4 Crucify
5 Icicle
6 Happy Phantom
7 God
8 Bells For Her
9 Me And A Gun
10 Baker Baker
11 Cornflake Girl
12 Tear In Your Hand
13 Summertime
14 Winter

Last Temptation Of Tori

Legend Of A Girl Child

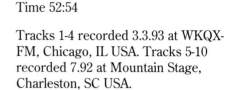

Vivid Sound VSP 51003
Time 52:54

Tracks 1-4 recorded 3.3.93 at WKQX-FM, Chicago, IL USA. Tracks 5-10 recorded 7.92 at Mountain Stage, Charleston, SC USA.

1 Crucify
2 Leather
3 Silent All These Years
4 Winter
5 Crucify
6 Silent All These Years
7 Happy Phantom
8 Me And A Gun
9 Winter
10 Smells Like Teen Spirit

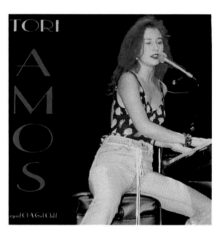

Legend Of A Girl Child

Little Earthquakes Demos and Outtakes

Collectors Pleasure COP 11
Time 55:47

1 Crucify
   outtake 4:14
2 Winter
   percussion mix 5:30
3 Happy Phantom
   outtake 3:20
4 Take To The Sky
   demo 4:20
5 Leather
   demo 3:16
6 Sarah Sylvia Cynthia Stout…
   outtake 2:34
7 Little Drummer Boy
   Promo 3:05
8 Crucify
   solo piano demo 5:23
9 Thoughts
   solo piano demo 2:46
10 Song for Eric
   outtake 1:13
11 Mary
   demo 4:20
12 Silent All These Years
   solo piano demo 3:35
13 Leather
   solo piano demo 3:14
14 The Pool
   demo 2:51
15 China
   solo piano demo 5:54

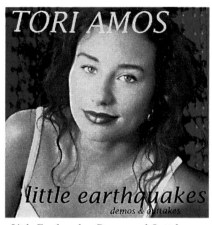

Little Earthquakes Demos and Outtakes

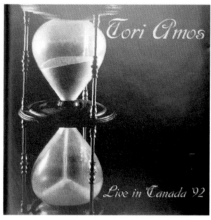

Live In Canada '92

Live In Canada '92

On Stage CD/ON 2303
Time 51:33

Recorded 2.28.92 from
Radio Broadcast, Toronto, Canada.

1 Happy Phantom
2 Crucify
3 Silent All These Years
4 Precious Things
5 Tear In Your Hand
6 Whole Lotta Love
7 Winter
8 Smells Like Teen Spirit
9 Silent All These Years

Little Rarities

Piano Classics PIC 01
Time 76:00

B-side compilation includes most B sides released up to the time.

1 Upside Down
2 Here. in My Head
3 Thank You
4 Angie
5 Flying Dutchman
6 Sugar
7 Sweet Dreams
8 Take To The Sky
9 Mary
10 Smells Like Teen Spirit
11 Humpty Dumpty
12 Thoughts
13 Song For Eric
14 Ode To The Banana King (Part One)
15 The Pool
16 The Happy Worker
17 Happy Phantom (Live)
18 Precious Things (Live)
19 Mother (Live)

Little Rarities

Live In Montreux 1992

Art Of Music AOM31102
Time 45:39

Source Unknown.

1 Little Earthquakes
2 Crucify
3 Silent All These Years
4 Precious Things
5 Happy Phantom
6 Whole Lotta Love
7 Me And A Gun
8 Winter
9 Smells Like Teens Spirit

Live In Montreux 1992

Magic

Snow 012/13
Time 65:47

Recorded 4.13.96 at
University Of Central Florida,
Orlando, FL USA.

1 Horses
2 Cornflake Girl
3 Doughnut Song
4 Love Song
5 Not The Red Baron
6 Flying Dutchman
7 Father Lucifer
8 Winter
9 In The Springtime Of His
  Voodoo
10 Cloud On My Tongue
11 Hey Jupiter

A Message For Your Heart

Red Phantom RPCD 1154
Time 51:53

Recorded from Radio Broadcast 10.28.92,
Toronto, Canada.

1 Happy Phantom
2 Crucify
3 Silent All These Years
4 Precious Things
5 Tear In Your Hand
6 Whole Lotta Love
7 Winter
8 Smells Like Teen Spirit
9 Silent All These Years

A Message For Your Heart

Magic

Me And A Piano

Flashback 01.94.0227
Time 68:48

Recorded 8.29.92 at
Moore Theater, Seattle, WA USA.

1 War
2 Crucify
3 Precious Things
4 Happy Phantom
5 Leather
6 Here. in My Head
7 Little Earthquakes
8 Whole Lotta Love
9 Thank You
10 Me And A Gun
11 Winter
12 Smells Like Teen Spirit
13 Mother
14 Tear In Your Hand
15 Song For Eric

Me And A Piano

Milan 1994

Milan 1994

Live Storm LSCD 51572
Time 72:16

Recorded 4.18.94 at Nacionalle, Milan,
Italy. Same show as *American
Heartbreaker* and *Milan 04.18.94*.

1 Crucify
2 Icicle
3 Precious Things
4 Leather
5 God
6 Silent All These Years
7 The Waitress
8 Here. in My Head
9 Baker Baker
10 Cornflake Girl
11 American Pie
12 Smells Like Teen Spirit
13 Past The Mission
14 Winter

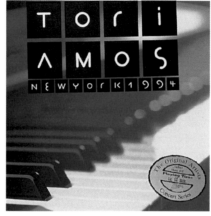
New York 1994

New York 1994

Arriba! ARR 94.078
Time 62:50

Recorded 3.30.94 at Symphony Space,
New York, NY USA.

1 Precious Things
2 Happy Phantom
3 Pretty Good Year
4 Flying Dutchman
5 Crucify
6 Icicle
7 Baker Baker
8 Cornflake Girl
9 Here. in My Head
10 Silent All These Years
11 The Waitress
12 Smells Like Teen Spirit

Now, Here, Nowhere

Teddy Bear TB87
Time 75:43

Recorded 8.11.94 at
The Orpheum Theater, New Orleans, LA
USA.

1 Sugar
2 Crucify
3 Icicle
4 Precious Things
5 Happy Phantom
6 Pretty Good Year
7 God
8 Silent All These Years
9 The Waitress
10 Leather
11 Me And A Gun
12 Baker Baker
13 Cornflake Girl
14 Winter

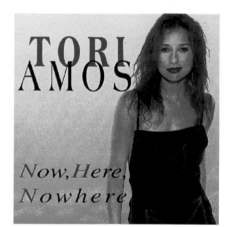
Now, Here, Nowhere

On Tour

High Live HL 2924
Time 67:43

Recorded from 1993 Radio Broadcast, Toronto, Canada. Same as *L'Affaire D' Amoreuse* and *The Piano*.

1 Smells Like Teen Spirit
2 Happy Phantom
3 Crucify
4 Silent All These Years
5 Precious Things
6 Leather
7 Tear In Your Hand
8 Whole Lotta Love
9 Little Earthquakes
10 Angie
11 Me And A Gun
12 China
13 Mother

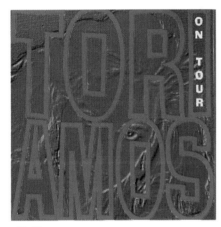

On Tour

Over The Pink

Amos 952
Time 71:06

B-sides and remixes from *Under The Pink*.

1 Honey
2 Black Swan
3 Home On The Range
  (with Cherokee addition)
4 Daisy Dead Petals
5 God (Dharma Kaya Mix)
6 God (Rainforest Resort Mix)
7 God (Thinking Mix)
8 Sister Janet
9 All The Girls Hate Her
10 Over It
11 A Case Of You
12 If 6 Was 9
13 Strange Fruit

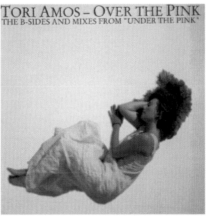

Over The Pink

Perfect Girl

Dead Dog Records SE449
Time 74:11

Recorded 6.15.94 at The Beacon Theater, New York, NY USA.

1 Leather
2 Crucify
3 Icicle
4 Precious Things
5 God
6 Silent All These Years
7 Pretty Good Year
8 The Waitress
9 Bells For Her
10 Me And A Gun
11 Winter
12 Cornflake Girl
13 American Pie
14 Smells Like Teen Spirit

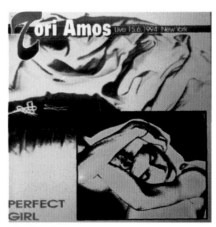

Perfect Girl

The Piano

Lunatic LU 2005
Time 67:43

Recorded from 1993 Radio Broadcast, Toronto, Canada. Same as *L'Affaire D'Amoreuse* and *On Tour*.

1 Smells Like Teen Spirit
2 Happy Phantom
3 Crucify
4 Silent All These Years
5 Precious Things
6 Leather
7 Tear In Your Hand
8 Whole Lotta Love
9 Little Earthquakes
10 Angie
11 Me And A Gun
12 China
13 Mother

The Piano

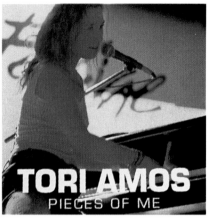

Pieces Of Me

Piano Girl Up North

Home Records HR6049-2
Time 64:44

Recorded 11.8.94 at St. Denis Theater, Montreal, Canada.

1 Leather
2 Crucify
3 Icicle
4 Whole Lotta Love/ Thank You
5 God
6 Past The Mission
7 Me And A Gun
8 China
9 Cornflake Girl
10 Cloud On My Tongue
11 Bells For Her
12 Winter

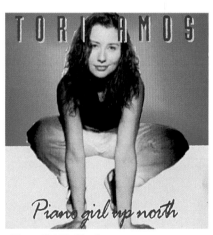

Piano Girl Up North

Pieces Of Me

Alley Kat AK010/11
Time 134:25
2-CD

CD 1: Tracks 1-9 and CD 2: Tracks 1-4 recorded at Alte Oper, Frankfurt, Germany.

CD 1:
1 Impromptu (New Shoes)/ Flying Dutchman
2 Crucify
3 Silent All These Years/ Precious Things
4 Leather
5 Whole Lotta Love/ Thank You/Upside Down/ Happy Phantom
6 China/Tear In Your Hand
7 Me And A Gun
8 Winter
9 Smells Like Teen Spirit

CD 2:
1 Mother
2 Sentimental Journey
3 Sugar
4 A Case Of You
5 Here. in My Head
   Moore Theater, Seattle, WA USA 8.29.92
6 Little Earthquakes
   Same As Above
7 Ain't No Sunshine
   Sunderland, UK 12.12.91
8 Mary
   St. Andrews Hall, Detroit, MI USA 10.30.92
9 Little Drummer Boy
   Anaconda Theater, Santa Barbara, CA USA 8.25.92
10 Imagine
   Sunderland, UK 12.12.91
11 Song For Eric
   Moore Theater, Seattle, WA USA 8.29.92
12 Girl
   Coach House, San Juan Capistrano, CA USA 9.5.95
13 Take To The Sky
   Count Basie Theater, Red Bank, NJ USA 10.11.92
14 Angie
   Stadpark, Hamburg, Germany 6.8.92

Popcorn Girl

Popcorn Girl

Shinola SH 69011
Time 64:03

Live In USA 1994.

1 Icicle
2 Crucify
3 Landslide
4 Leather
5 Precious Things
6 Space Dog
7 The Waitress
8 Me And A Gun
9 Leather
10 Silent All These Years
11 Bells For Her
12 Smells Like Teen Spirit
13 Cornflake Girl

Precious Little Diamonds

Primadonna PD118
73:43

B-sides, rarities, compilation and soundtrack cuts.

1 Talula (Tornado Mix)
2 Frog On My Toe
3 Sister Named Desire
4 Alamo
5 Talula (BT's Synethasia Mix)
6 Amazing Grace/'Til The Chicken
7 Famous Blue Raincoat
8 Losing My Religion
9 Butterfly
10 This Old Man
11 Hungarian Wedding Song
12 Toodles Mr. Jim
13 London Girls
14 That's What I Like Mick
   (The Sandwich Song)
15 Samurai
16 Baltimore
17 Walking With You

Precious Rarities

Sacem P910123
Time 55:49

B-sides, rarities and covers.

1 Here. in My Head
2 Little Drummer Boy
3 Upside Down
4 Sister Janet
5 Sarah Cynthia Sylvia Stout…
6 Heart Attack At 23
7 A Case Of You
8 Imagine
9 Sentimental Journey
10 Smells Like Teen Spirit
11 Angie
12 Whole Lotta Love
13 American Pie
14 Ain't No Sunshine

Precious Rarities

Purple Rose

Moonraker 084/85
Time 145:41
2-CD

CD 1: Tracks 1-13 and CD 2: Tracks 1-6 recorded 3.25.96 at Friedrichstadpalasat, Berlin, Germany. CD 2: Tracks 7-15 recorded 4.9.94 at Trinitatiskrine, Berlin, Germany. CD 2: Track 15 Radio Broadcast.

CD 1:
1 Beauty Queen/Horses
2 Leather
3 American Pie/Smells Like Teen Spirit
4 Marianne
5 Caught A Lite Sneeze
6 Little Amsterdam
7 Cornflake Girl
8 Doughnut Song
9 Bells For Her
10 Precious Things
11 Not The Red Baron
12 In The Springtime Of His Voodoo
13 Winter

CD 2:
1 Father Lucifer
2 Me And A Gun
3 If 6 Was 9
4 Putting The Damage On
5 Space Dog
6 Hey Jupiter
7 American Pie
8 Smells Like Teen Spirit
9 Crucify
10 Jesus My Saviour
11 Me And A Gun
12 Baker Baker
13 Cornflake Girl
14 Winter
15 Interview

Purple Rose

Precious Things

Precious Things

Star Spangled Music SSM002
Time 62:38

Recorded 4.29.94 at The Palladium, London, England.

1 American Pie
2 Smells Like Teen Spirit
3 Icicle
4 Crucify
5 Happy Phantom
6 God
7 Silent All These Years
8 Bells For Her
9 Winter
10 Cornflake Girl
11 China
12 Precious Things
   6.29.94: Late Show, New York, NY USA

Rhapsody In Pink

Alley Kat AK 040/41
Time 142:06
2-CD

CD 1: Tracks 1-14 and CD 2: Tracks 1-4 recorded 3.20.94 at Meany Hall, Seattle WA USA.

CD 1:
1 Sugar
2 Crucify
3 Icicle
4 Precious Things
5 Happy Phantom
6 Pretty Good Year
7 God
8 Silent All These Years
9 Past The Mission
10 The Waitress
11 Leather
12 Smells Like Teen Spirit
13 Me And A Gun
14 Baker Baker

CD 2:
1 Cornflake Girl
2 Tear In Your Hand
3 Winter
4 Song For Eric
5 Flying Dutchman
   Edinburgh, Scotland 2.28.94
6 Mother
   Eugene, OR USA 8.30.92
7 Bells For Her
   Glasgow, Scotland 2.27.94
8 Little Earthquakes
   Eugene, OR USA 8.30.92
9 Upside Down
   Eugene, OR USA 8.30.92
10 A Case Of You
   Los Angeles, CA USA 3.22.94
11 China
   Newcastle, England 2.15.94
12 God
   Los Angeles, CA USA 3..22.94
13 Icicle
   Los Angeles, CA USA 3.22.94
14 Baker Baker
   Los Angeles, CA USA 3.22.94

Rhapsody In Pink

Self Gratification

Self Gratification

Snow 018/2
Time 139:53
2-CD

CD 1: Tracks 1-15 and CD 2: Tracks 1-6
recorded 5.3.96 at Tower Theater,
Philadelphia, PA USA. CD 2: Tracks 7-14
recorded 8.16.92 at Carefree Theater,
West Palm Beach, FL USA.

CD 1:
1 Beauty Queen
2 Horses
3 Angie
4 Leather
5 Caught A Lite Sneeze
6 Cornflake Girl
7 Doughnut Song
8 Pretty Good Year
9 Mother
10 Mohammed My Friend
11 Precious Things
12 Not The Red Baron
13 Sweet Dreams
14 Bells For Her
15 Me And A Gun

CD 2:
1 Twinkle
2 Silent All These Years
3 Father Lucifer
4 Tubular Bells/Smalltown Boy
5 Cloud On My Tongue
6 Hey Jupiter
7 Upside Down
8 Me And A Gun
9 Winter
10 Assholes Are Cheap Today
11 Smells Like Teen Spirit
12 Mother
13 China
14 Girl

Savior Beneath These Dirty Sheets

Savior Beneath These Dirty Sheets

ROLA Rola 20
Time 79:30

Recorded Live at various locations in the
US and Canada 1992/1993.

1 Happy Phantom
2 Crucify
3 Silent All These Years
4 Precious Things
5 Leather
6 Tear In Your Hand
7 Whole Lotta Love
8 Smells Like Teen Spirit
9 Winter
10 Girl
11 China
12 Mother
13 Little Earthquakes
14 Angie
15 Me And A Gun

Sellout

Sellout

Snow 004/5
Time 102:04
2-CD

Recorded 4.9.96 at Tampa Bay Performing Arts Center, Tampa, FL USA.

CD 1:
1 Beauty Queen
2 Horses
3 Crucify
4 Losing My Religion
5 Mohammed My Friend
6 Bells For Her
7 Little Amsterdam
8 Cornflake Girl
9 Space Dog
10 Doughnut Song
11 Leather
12 Precious Things
13 Not The Red Baron

CD 2:
1 Flying Dutchman
2 Caught A Lite Sneeze
3 Me And A Gun
4 Putting The Damage On
5 Winter
6 Take To The Sky
7 In The Springtime Of His Voodoo
8 Hey Jupiter

Silent All These Years

Living Legend LLRCD 245
Time 64:46

Tracks 1-9 recorded 1992 in Montreux, Switzerland. Tracks 10-12 recorded 9.4/5.92 in San Juan Capistrano, CA USA. Track 13 recorded 10.28.92 in Toronto, Canada all from radio broadcasts.

1 Little Earthquakes
2 Crucify
3 Silent All These Years
4 Precious Things
5 Happy Phantom
6 Whole Lotta Love
7 Me And A Gun
8 Winter
9 Smells Like Teen Spirit
10 Girl
11 Leather
12 China
13 Tear In Your Hand

Silent All These Years

Silent All These Years

Live Line LL 15353
Time 75:56

Tracks 1-8 recorded 9.4/5.92 at The Coach House, San Juan Capistrano, CA USA. Tracks 9-15 recorded 10.28.92 from Radio Broadcast, Toronto, Canada.

1 Crucify
2 Silent All These Years
3 Happy Phantom
4 Girl
5 Whole Lotta Love
6 Leather
7 Smells Like Teen Spirit
8 China
9 Crucify
10 Silent All These Years
11 Precious Things
12 Tear In Your Hand
13 Whole Lotta Love/ Thank You
14 Winter
15 Smells Like Teen Spirit

Silent All These Years

Space Doggin' Bruins

Strangled Records STR006/7
Time 120:32
2-CD

CD 1: Tracks 1-13 and CD 2: Tracks 1-5
recorded 3.22.94 at Wadsworth Theater
UCLA Campus, Los Angeles, CA USA.

CD 1:
1 Sugar
2 Crucify
3 Icicle
4 Precious Things
5 Happy Phantom
6 Pretty Good Year
7 God
8 Silent All These Years
9 Past The Mission
10 The Waitress
11 Smells Like Teen Spirit
12 Me And A Gun
13 Baker Baker

CD 2:
1 Cornflake Girl
2 Winter
3 China
4 All The Girls Hate Her
5 Cloud On My Tongue
6 Take To The Sky
   New Jersey 10.11.92
7 Little Earthquakes
   Seattle 8.29.92
8 Girl
   San Juan Capistrano 9.5.92
9 Mary
   Detroit 10.30.92
10 Imagine
   UK 12.12.92
11 Angie
   Germany 6.8.92

Space Doggin' Bruins

Spirit In The Sky

Kiss The Stone KTS 235
Time 77:01

Recorded 3.29/30.94 at Symphony
Space, New York, NY USA.

1 Flying Dutchman
2 Crucify
3 Icicle
4 Precious Things
5 Happy Phantom
6 Pretty Good Year
7 God
8 Silent All These Years
9 The Waitress
10 Smells Like Teen Spirit
11 Baker Baker
12 Cornflake Girl
13 Here. in My Head
14 God
15 Baker Baker
16 Cornflake Girl
17 Pretty Good Year

Spirit In The Sky

Sugar Baby

Banzi BZCD 042
Time 77:17

Recorded 9.1.94 at The Orpheum
Theater, San Francisco, CA USA.

1 Crucify
2 Space Dog
3 Precious Things
4 Icicle
5 God
6 China
7 The Waitress
8 Bells For Her
9 Baker Baker
10 Cornflake Girl
11 Silent All These Years
12 Past The Mission
13 A Case Of You
14 American Pie
15 Smells Like Teen Spirit

Sugar Baby

Sweet Dreams Are Made Of This

RTW RTW 014
Time 67:19

Recorded 3.30.94 at Symphony Space, New York, NY USA.

1 Flying Dutchman
2 Crucify
3 Icicle
4 Precious Things
5 Happy Phantom
6 Pretty Good Year
7 God
8 Silent All These Years
9 The Waitress
10 Smells Like Teen Spirit
11 Baker Baker
12 Cornflake Girl
13 Here. in My Head

Sweet Dreams Are Made Of This

Sweet Old England

RUPERT 9692/3
Time 106:56
2-CD

Recorded 3.9.96 at The Royal Albert Hall, London, England.

CD 1:
1 Intro
2 Beauty Queen
3 Horses
4 Crucify
5 Smells Like Teen Spirit
6 Marianne
7 Bells For Her
8 Little Amsterdam
9 Way Down/Space Dog
10 Cornflake Girl
11 Doughnut Song
12 Leather

CD 2:
1 Precious Things
2 Not The Red Baron
3 Blood Roses
4 Winter
5 Me And A Gun
6 Putting The Damage On
7 China
8 Past The Mission
9 Baker Baker
10 Sweet England
11 Hey Jupiter

Sweet Old England

Teen Spirit

International Broadcast Recordings
IBR2335
Time 52:51

Tracks 1-4 recorded 3.3.93 at WKQX-FM, Chicago, IL USA. Tracks 5-10 recorded 7.92 at Mountain Stage, Charleston, SC USA. This CD is the same as *Legend Of A Girl Child* CD.

1 Crucify
2 Leather
3 Silent All These Years
4 Winter
5 Crucify
6 Silent All These Years
7 Happy Phantom
8 Me And A Gun
9 Winter
10 Smells Like Teen Spirit

Teen Spirit

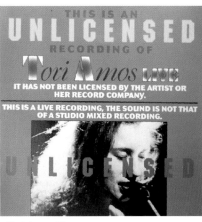

Tori Amos Live

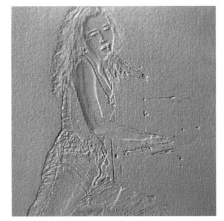

Tori Amos

Thank You Angie

Thank You Angie

International Broadcast Recordings
IBR2495
Time 76:35

Recorded 11.8.92 at Page Hall, Albany,
NY USA.

1 Crucify
2 Silent All These Years
3 Precious Things
4 Happy Phantom
5 Leather
6 Tear In Your Hand
7 Whole Lotta Love
8 Thank You
9 Me And A Gun
10 Winter
11 Smells Like Teen Spirit
12 China
13 Angie

Tori Amos

PR Records imm 40.90313
Time 54:00

Recorded 1992 in Washington, Florida,
California, Maryland, San Juan and
Toronto. 1994 in New York.

1 Crucify
2 Leather
3 Smells Like Teen Spirit
4 Silent All These Years
5 China
6 Happy Phantom
7 Whole Lotta Love
8 Girl
9 Baker Baker
10 Cornflake Girl
11 God
12 Pretty Good Year
13 Little Drummer Boy

Tori Amos Live

Mainline SW138
Time 46:25

Recorded from Radio Broadcast 10.28.92,
Toronto, Canada.

1 Happy Phantom
2 Crucify
3 Silent All These Years
4 Precious Things
5 Tear In Your Hand
6 Whole Lotta Love
7 Winter
8 Smells Like Teen Spirit
9 Silent All These Years

Tori Stories

Tori And Her Mask

Tornado TOR-005/006
Time 148:43
2-CD

Recorded 8.3.94 at Tampa Theater, Tampa, FL USA (two Shows). CD 1: Tracks 1-13 and CD 2: Tracks 1-3 (1st Show). CD 2: Tracks 4-13 (2nd Show).

CD 1:
1 Leather
2 Precious Things
3 Pretty Good Year
4 Crucify
5 The Waitress
6 God
7 Sugar
8 Yes, Anastasia
9 Me And A Gun
10 Angie
11 Cornflake Girl
12 China
13 Wrapped Around Your Finger

CD 2:
1 Cloud On My Tongue
2 Bells For Her
3 O' Danny Boy
4 Little Earthquakes
5 Happy Phantom
6 Icicle
7 American Pie
8 Smells Like Teen Spirit
9 Space Dog
10 Baker Baker
11 Silent All These Years
12 Landslide
13 Winter

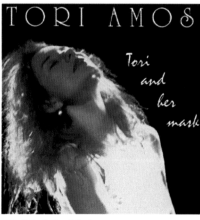

Tori And Her Mask

Tori Stories

Primadonna PD100/101/102/103
Time 290:29
4CD

CD 1: Tracks 1 & 2 from *Baltimore* 7" single. Track 3 outtake from *Baltimore* sessions. Tracks 4-7 *Under The Pink* Demos. Tracks 8-13 from wedding in Spring of 1978 as Tori's father presides. Track 14 *A Conversation With God* (*Atilla The Honey*). CD 2 recorded 3.15.92 at The Roxy Theater, Amsterdam, Holland. CD 3 (see below). CD 4: Tracks 1-11 recorded 3.29.94 at Palladium, London, England. Tracks 12-14 recorded 3.14.92 Amsterdam, Holland.

CD 1:
1 Baltimore
2 Walking With You
3 A Happy Day
4 Icicle
5 Cloud On My Tongue
6 Baker Baker
7 Pretty Good Year/Honey
8 Piano Improvisation
9 Evergreen
10 If
11 You Needed Me
12 You Light Up My Life
13 We've Only Just Begun
14 Atilla The Honey

CD 2:
1 Crucify
2 Silent All These Years
3 Precious Things
4 Happy Phantom
5 Leather
6 Upside Down
7 Little Earthquakes
8 Whole Lotta Love
9 Thank You
10 Me And A Gun
11 Winter
12 Smells Like Teen Spirit
13 Mother
14 China
15 Song For Eric

CD 3:

1 Purple Rain
  Mt. Baker Theater, Bellingham, WA USA 9.15.94
2 Honey
  Opera House, Seattle, WA USA 9.14.94
3 Landslide
  Tampa Theater, Tampa, FL USA 8.4.94
4 Wrapped Around Your Finger
  Majestic Theater, Dallas, TX USA 8.14.94
5 Danny Boy
  Majestic Theater, Dallas, TX USA 8.14.94
6 Black Swan
  Mt. Baker Theater, Bellingham, WA USA 9.15.94
7 Famous Blue Raincoat
  Fulton Theater, Pittsburgh, PA USA 7.1.94
8 I'm On Fire
  Palace Theater, New Haven, CT USA 10.26.94
9 Sister Janet
  Zellerbach Auditorium, Berkeley, CA USA 9.10.94
10 For Emily Whenever I May…
  Guildhall, Portsmouth, England 4.21.94
11 Yes, Anastasia
  Palladium, London, England 4.30.94
12 Take To The Sky
  Orpheum, San Francisco, CA USA 8.31.94
13 Saturday Afternoons 1963
  Barbicon Center, York, England 4.24.94
14 Daisy Dead Petals
  Orpheum, San Francisco, CA USA 8.31.94
15 Boys In The Trees
  Barrymore Theater, Madison, WI USA 7.11.94
16 She's Leaving Home
  Hult Center, Eugene, OR USA 9.12.94

CD 4:

1 American Pie
2 Smells Like Teen Spirit
3 Icicle
4 Crucify
5 Happy Phantom
6 God
7 Silent All These Years
8 Bells For Her
9 Winter
10 Cornflake Girl
11 China
12 Crucify
13 Leather
14 China

Tori's Choice

Tori The Fox

Tori The Fox

Rocks 92129
Time 76:55

Recorded 4.1.94 at Center Stage, Atlanta, GA USA.

1 Sugar
2 Crucify
3 Icicle
4 Precious Things
5 Happy Phantom
6 Pretty Good Year
7 God
8 Silent All These Years
9 The Waitress
10 Leather
11 Me And A Gun
12 Baker Baker
13 Cornflake Girl
14 Winter

Tori's Choice

Hurricane 55/56
Time 148:51
2-CD

CD 1: Tracks 1-13 and CD 2: Tracks 1-7 recorded 5.2.96 at Tower Theater, Philadelphia, PA USA. CD 2: Tracks 8-14 recorded 8.8.92 at Carefree Theater, West Palm Beach, FL USA.

CD 1:

1 Beauty Queen
2 Horses
3 Yes, Anastasia
4 Blood Roses
5 Little Amsterdam
6 Cornflake Girl
7 Doughnut Song
8 Pretty Good Year
9 Love Song
10 Precious Things
11 Not The Red Baron
12 Caught A Lite Sneeze
13 Icicle

CD 2:

1 Talula
2 Me And A Gun
3 Winter
4 Somewhere Over The Rainbow
5 Past The Mission
6 Here. in My Head
7 Hey Jupiter
8 Little Earthquakes
9 Crucify
10 Silent All These Years
11 Precious Things
12 Happy Phantom
13 Leather
14 Whole Lotta Love

Toronto 1992

Live Storm LSCD51554
Time 51:29

Recorded 10.28.92 at The Phoenix Club, Toronto, Canada.

Same as *Message For Your Heart* CD.

1 Happy Phantom
2 Crucify
3 Silent All These Years
4 Precious Things
5 Tear In Your Hand
6 Whole Lotta Love
7 Winter
8 Smells Like Teen Spirit
9 Silent All These Years

Toronto 1992

Ultra Rare Tori

Androgynous/Blue Moon Music
AR4/BM2

Tracks 1-10 from *Y Kant Tori Read*.
Tracks 11-14 live cover versions 1991-94.
Track 15 from *We've Got Your Yule Logs Hangin'*. Track 16 from *Speaking Of Christmas and Other Things*. Track 17 from *Ruby Trax*.

1 The Big Picture
2 Cool On Your Island
3 Fayth
4 Fire On The Side
5 Pirates
6 Floating City
7 Heart Attack At 23
8 On The Boundary
9 You Go To My Head
10 Etienne Trilogy
  A) The Highlands
  B) Etienne
  C) Sky Boat Song
11 Ain't No Sunshine
12 A Case Of You
13 Imagine
14 Sentimental Journey
15 Little Drummer Boy
16 Sarah Cynthia Sylvia Stout…
17 Ring My Bell

Ultra Rare Tori

Under The Covers

Under The Covers

TA TA1001
Time 70:00

1 Ain't No Sunshine
  12.91 Suderland UK
2 Imagine
  12.91 Suderland UK
3 Sentimental Journey
  6.7.92 Frankfurt, Germany
4 A Case Of You
  6.7.92 Frankfurt, Germany
5 Whole Lotta Love/
  Thank You
  9.29.92 Boulder, CO USA
6 Love Song
  1.19.93 KROQ Radio, Los Angeles, CA USA
7 Home On The Range
  3.6.94 London, England
8 Famous Blue Raincoat
  3.6.94 London, England
9 Tuesday Afternoon
  3.16.94 Capitol Radio, London England
10 Angie
  3.16.94 Capitol Radio, London England
11 American Pie
  4.9.94 Berlin, Germany
  (Night Of Kurt Cobain's Suicide)
12 Smells Like Teen Spirit
  4.9.94 Berlin, Germany (as above)
13 Summertime
  4.9.94 Berlin, Germany (as above)
14 Candle In The Wind
  8.3.94 Tampa, FL USA
15 Wrapped Around Your Finger
  10.16.94 East Lansing, MI USA
16 With A Little Help From My Friends
  10.16.94 East Lansing, MI USA
17 Landslide
  10.16.94 East Lansing, MI USA
18 I'm On Fire
  10.16.94 East Lansing, MI USA

Under The Pink Tour 1994

Piano Classics PIC002/3
Time 149:55
2-CD

CD 1: Tracks 1-17 and CD 2: tracks 1-3 recorded 4.10.94 at CCH2, Hamburg, Germany. CD 2: Tracks 4-14 recorded 6.8.92 at Stadpark, Hamburg, Germany.

CD 1:
1 Intro (Rawhide)
2 Space Dog
3 Crucify
4 Another story about her grandmother
5 Icicle
6 Precious Things
7 Happy Phantom
8 Story about Past The Mission
9 Past The Mission
10 God
11 Silent All These Years
12 The Waitress
13 Leather
14 Bells For Her
15 Me And A Gun
16 Winter
17 Cornflake Girl

CD 2:
1 Tear In Your Hand
2 Smells Like Teen Spirit
3 Pretty Good Year
4 Song For Eric
5 Flying Dutchman
6 Crucify
7 Whole Lotta Love/ Thank You
8 Silent All These Years
9 Precious Things
10 Happy Phantom
11 Smells Like Teen Spirit
12 Leather
13 Angie
14 Sugar
15 Mother

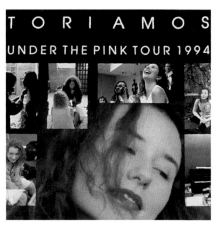

Under The Pink Tour 1994

Unplugged Girl

Blizzard BLZD154
Time 72:27

Tracks 1-8 recorded 4.11.96 at The Majestic Theater, New York, NY USA. Track 9 recorded 1992 Saturday Night Live Rehearsal, New York, NY USA.

1 Cornflake Girl
2 Blood Roses
3 Silent All These Years
4 Icicle
5 Caught A Lite Sneeze
6 Over The Rainbow
7 Hey Jupiter
8 In The Springtime Of His Voodoo
9 Crucify

Unplugged Girl

Unreadable Tori And Other Rarities

Tornado TOR004

Tracks 1-10 from *Y Kant Tori Read.*
Tracks 11-16 B-Sides And Rarities.

1 The Big Picture
2 Cool On Your Island
3 Fayth
4 Fire On The Side
5 Pirates
6 Floating City
7 Heart Attack At 23
8 On The Boundary
9 You Go To My Head
10 Etienne Trilogy
  A) The Highlands
  B) Etienne
  C) Skyeboat Song
11 Ode To The Banana King (Part One)
12 Song For Eric
13 Happy Phantom
14 Ring My Bell
15 The Happy Worker
16 Workers

The Unreadable Tori And Other Rarities

Upside Down

Vandelay Industries LTX CD001
Time 144:58
2-CD

B-Sides and rarities collection.

CD 1:
1 The Pool
2 Upside Down
3 Mary
4 Sugar
5 Sister Janet
6 Take To The Sky
7 Sweet Dreams
8 Home On The Range
9 Humpty Dumpty
10 Flying Dutchman
11 Ode To The Banana King (Part One)
12 Here. in My Head
13 Daisy Dead Petals
14 Honey
15 Black Swan
16 Thoughts
17 All The Girls Hate Her
18 Over It
19 Song For Eric

CD 2:
1 A Case Of You
2 If 6 Was 9
3 Strange Fruit
4 Thank You
5 Angie
6 Smells Like Teen Spirit
7 Ring My Bell
8 Flying Dutchman (Live)
9 Icicle (Live)
10 Past The Mission (Live)
11 Whole Lotta Love/
   Thank You (Live)
12 Here. in My Head (Live)
13 Little Drummer Boy (Live)
14 Famous Blue Raincoat (Live)
15 Upside Down (Live)

Upside Down

Voices In The Air

Snow SNOW002/3
114:39

CD 1: Tracks 1-11 and CD 2: Tracks 1-7 recorded 4.10.96 at PAC, Gainesville, FL USA. CD 2: Tracks 8-13 B-sides.

CD 1:
1 Beauty Queen/Horses
2 Mr. Zebra
3 Little Earthquakes
4 Bells For Her
5 Little Amsterdam
6 Cornflake Girl
7 Doughnut Song
8 In The Springtime Of His Voodoo
9 Silent All These Years
10 Precious Things
11 Not The Red Baron

CD 2:
1 Caught A Lite Sneeze
2 Me And A Gun
3 Twinkle
4 A Case Of You
5 Tear In Your Hand
6 Sugar
7 Hey Jupiter
8 This Old Man
9 London Girls
10 Hungarian Wedding Song
11 That's What I Like Mick
12 Toodles, Mr. Jim
13 Samurai

White Horses

ReaLive RLCD34
Time 74:11

Recorded 9.29.92 at The Boulder Theater, Boulder, CO USA.

1 Crucify
2 Silent All These Years
3 Precious Things
4 Happy Phantom
5 Leather
6 Upside Down
7 Little Earthquakes
8 Whole Lotta Love
9 Me And A Gun
10 Winter
11 Smells Like Teen Spirit
12 Mother
13 China
14 Song For Eric

White Horses

Voices In The Air

Wild Horses

TSUNAMI TSO2
Time 53:88

Tracks 1 & 2 recorded 1.20.96 from Saturday Night Live. Tracks 3 & 4 recorded 1.21.96 at MTV Studios. Tracks 5-8 recorded 1.4.96 from Modern Rock Live. Track 9 recorded 2.2.96 from Regis & Kathy Lee. Track 10 recorded 2.8.96 from Tonight Show. Tracks 11-14 recorded 8.2.96 from Northwest Airlines Lounge, Minneapolis, MN USA.

1 Caught A Lite Sneeze
2 Hey Jupiter
3 Doughnut Song
4 Horses
5 From Mark
6 Putting The Damage On
7 Losing My Religion
8 Leather
9 Putting The Damage On
10 Caught A Lite Sneeze
11 Crucify
12 Silent All These Years
13 Happy Phantom
14 Tori Speaks

Wild Horses

Winter

Teddy Bear Records TB44
Time 65:30

Recorded 9.29.92 at The Boulder Theater, Boulder, CO USA.

1 Crucify
2 Silent All These Years
3 Precious Things
4 Happy Phantom
5 Leather
6 Upside Down
7 Little Earthquakes
8 Whole Lotta Love
9 Winter
10 Smells Like Teen Spirit
11 Mother
12 China
13 Song For Eric

Winter

Whole Lotta Teen Spirit

RSM RSM024
Time 39:03

Recorded 9.5.92 at The Coach House, San Juan Capistrano, CA USA.

1 Crucify
2 Silent All These Years
3 Happy Phantom
4 Girl
5 Whole Lotta Love
6 Leather
7 Smells Like Teen Spirit
8 China

Whole Lotta Teen Spirit

A Woman On A Mission

Home Records HR 5931-8
Time 70:55

Recorded 4.19.94 at
The Palladium, Rome, Italy

1 American Pie
2 Smells Like Teen Spirit
3 Crucify
4 Icicle
5 Precious Things
6 Leather
7 God
8 Cornflake Girl
9 Pretty Good Year
10 Flying Dutchman
11 China
12 Angie
13 Me And A Gun
14 Mother
15 Happy Phantom

A Woman On A Mission

Y Kant Tori Read

Atlantic Atlantic 81845-1
German Bootleg
Time 47:19

This CD can be easily distinguished
from the real CD by the number. In the
artwork the number 81845-1 is used, the
suffix 1 is the universal standard for LPs.
CDs always end with the number 2.
Also, the spine of the CD is black with
white printing. Real Atlantic CDs are
white with red printing.

1 The Big Picture
2 Cool On Your Island
3 Fayth
4 Fire On The Side
5 Pirates
6 Floating City
7 Heart Attack At 23
8 On The Boundary
9 You Go To My Head
10 Etienne Trilogy
   A) The Highlands
   B) Etienne
   C) Skyeboat Song

Y Kant Tori Read: German Bootleg (Front)

Y Kant Tori Read: German Bootleg (Back)

Y Kant Tori Read

Y Kant Tori Read

Atlantic Atlantic 81845-1
German Bootleg
Time 47:19

Same CD as above except cover is from
Cool On Your Island 7" single.

1 The Big Picture
2 Cool On Your Island
3 Fayth
4 Fire On The Side
5 Pirates
6 Floating City
7 Heart Attack At 23
8 On The Boundary
9 You Go To My Head
10 Etienne Trilogy
   A) The Highlands
   B) Etienne
   C) Skyeboat Song

Y Kant Tori
Read And
Other Rarities

Pacific Recording Corporation 001

Tracks 1-10 From *Y Kant Tori Read.*
Tracks 11-13 from *Silent All These Years*
UK Limited CD single. Track 14 from
Ruby Trax compilation. Tracks 15-16
from *Toys* Soundtrack.

1 The Big Picture
2 Cool On Your Island
3 Fayth
4 Fire On The Side
5 Pirates
6 Floating City
7 Heart Attack At 23
8 On The Boundary
9 You Go To My Head
10 Etienne Trilogy
  A) The Highlands
  B) Etienne
  C) Skyboat Song
11 Ode To The Banana King
  (Part One)
12 Song For Eric
13 Happy Phantom (Live)
14 Ring My Bell
15 The Happy Worker
16 Workers

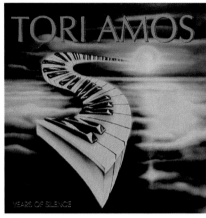

Years Of Silence

Years Of
Silence

CDM G-53 240
Time 46:35

1 Happy Phantom
2 Silent All These Years
3 Crucify
4 Precious Things
5 Tear In Your Hand
6 Girl
7 Whole Lotta Love
8 Leather
9 China
10 Smells Like Teen Spirit

Y Kant Tori Read And Other Rarities
(Front)

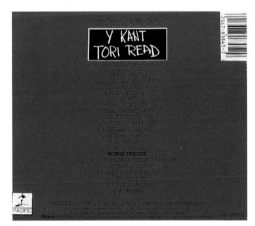

Y Kant Tori Read And Other Rarities
(Back)

bootleg videos Compilamos Grace

Compilamos

1 Butterfly
   Tonight Show 2.25.95
2 Cloud On My Tongue
   Greg Kinnear 8.25.94
3 Winter
   Night After Night 1992
4 Crucify
   MTV 1992
5 Icicle
   MTV Alternative Nation 1992
6 Precious Things
   David Letterman 6.28.94
7 Cornflake Girl
   Conan O' Brien 6.28.94
8 Me And A Gun/
   Crucify
   Dini Petty Show 1992
9 Crucify
   Top Of The Pops 1992
10 The Big Picture
   Atlantic Promo Video
11 Past The Mission/
   China
   French TV
12 Pretty Good Year
   Top Of The Pops 1994
13 God/Baker Baker
   Tonight Show 2.12.94
14 Pretty Good Year
   Good Morning America 3.30.94
15 Cornflake Girl
   David Letterman 3.28.94
16 Silent All These Years/Crucify
   Dennis Miller Show 5.12.92
17 Crucify
   David Letterman 5.92
18 Crucify/Winter
   Tonight Show 1.12.93
19 Crucify
   CBS This Morning 9.9.92
20 Silent All These Years
   Arsenio Hall 9.10.92

Grace

Recorded 11.8.94 at St. Denis, Montreal, Canada.

1 Leather
2 Crucify
3 Icicle
4 Whole Lotta Love
5 God
6 Past The Mission
7 Me And A Gun
8 China
9 Cornflake Girl
10 Cloud On My Tongue
11 Bells For Her
12 Winter

Compilamos

Compilamos (Repackaged)

Grace (Original)

Grace (Repackaged)

Sunshine

Recorded 4.12.96 at Sunrise Theater,
Ft. Lauderdale FL, USA

1 Beauty Queen/Horses
2 American Pie
3 Smells Like Teen Spirit
4 Happy Phantom
5 Blood Roses
6 Little Amsterdam
7 Cornflake Girl
8 Doughnut Song
9 In The Springtime Of His
  Voodoo
10 Silent All These Years
11 Precious Things
12 Not The Red Baron
13 Crucify
14 Marianne
15 Caught A Lite Sneeze
16 Me And A Gun
17 Putting The Damage On
18 Thank You
19 Tear In Your Hand
20 Here. in My Head
21 Hey Jupiter

Tori Amos: Albany, NY USA… November 18th, 1992

1 Crucify
2 Silent All These Years
3 Precious Things
4 Happy Phantom
5 Leather
6 Tear In Your Hand
7 Whole Lotta Love
8 Thank You
9 Me And A Gun
10 Winter
11 Smells Like Teen Spirit
12 China
13 Angie

Tori Amos: Baltimore, MD USA… July 25th, 1994

Recorded 7.25.94 at Meyerhoff
Symphony Hall, Baltimore MD, USA.

1 Little Earthquakes
2 Leather
3 Icicle
4 Precious Things
5 Space Dog
6 God
7 Silent All These Years
8 The Waitress
9 Bells For Her
10 Me And A Gun
11 Angie
12 Cornflake Girl
13 American Pie
14 Smells Like Teen Spirit
15 Pretty Good Year
16 China
17 Landslide
18 Winter

Sunshine

Tori Amos: Albany, NY USA…
November 18th, 1992

Tori Amos: Baltimore, MD USA…
July 25th, 1994

Tori Amos: Live In NY 1992

Source Unknown.

1 Mary
2 Crucify
3 Silent All These Years
4 Precious Things
5 Happy Phantom
6 Tori Tells A Story
7 Leather
8 Tear In Your Hand
9 Upside Down
10 Whole Lotta Love
11 Me And A Gun
12 Winter
13 Smells Like Teen Spirit
14 China
15 Here. in My Head
16 Angie

Under The Pink

Recorded 11.8.94 at St. Denis, Montreal, Canada. Same as *Grace* video.

1 Leather
2 Crucify
3 Icicle
4 Whole Lotta Love
5 God
6 Past The Mission
7 Me And A Gun
8 China
9 Cornflake Girl
10 Cloud On My Tongue
11 Bells For Her
12 Winter

Tori Amos: Live In NY 1992

Under The Pink

chapter nine
tour dates

Little Earthquakes Tour 1992

January 1992

29 London, England
Shaw Theatre

30 London, England
Shaw Theatre

February 1992

7 Liverpool, England
Blue Coat Arts Centre

8 Hanley, England
Arts Centre

9 Reading, England
University

11 Middleboro, England
Arena

13 Glasgow, Scotland
King Tut's

14 Edinburgh, Scotland
Music Box

15 Newcastle, England
River Side

16 Nottingham, England
Polytechnic

17 Manchester, England
University

19 Norwich, England
Arts Centre

20 Hull, England
Spring St. Theatre

21 Sheffield, England
University

March 1992

7 Frankfurt, Germany
Opera House

9 Munich, Germany
Kaffe Giesing

10 Berlin, Germany
Floz

11 Hamburg, Germany
Market Hall

15 Amsterdam, Holland
Roxy

16 Rome, Italy
Dal Big Mama

April 1992

2 London, England
London Royalty Theatre

3 London, England
London Royalty Theatre

5 Cambridge, England
Corn Exchange

7 Edinburgh, Scotland
Queen's Hall

10 Manchester, England
Free Trade Hall

11 Birmingham, England
Town Hall

20 New York, NY USA
Bottom Line

21 Pontiac, MI USA
Industry

22 Alexandria, VA USA
Birchmere

23 Pontiac, MI USA
Industry

24 Philadelphia, PA USA
Theater of Living Arts

25 Toronto, Ontario Canada
Rivoli's

27 Northampton, MA USA
Iron Horse Music Hall

28 Cambridge, MA USA
Night Stage

29 Chicago, IL USA
Schubas

30 Dallas, TX USA
Deep Ellum Live

May 1992

1 Houston, TX USA
Rockefeller

3 Minneapolis, MN USA
Fine Line Music Café

4 Atlanta, GA USA
The Point

6 Seattle, WA USA
Backstage

7 Vancouver, BC Canada
Cultural Center

8 Denver, CO USA
The Garage

9 San Francisco, CA USA
Bimbo's

10 San Diego, CA USA
Sound FX

11 Los Angeles, CA USA
The Roxy

23 Melbourne, Australia
Brash's

25 Sydney, Australia
Rose, Shamrock & Thistle

30 Taipei, Taiwan
Pablo

June 1992

6 Hockenheim, Germany
Rockam Ring

7 Frankfurt, Germany
Alte Oper

8 Hamburg, Germany
Stadpark

9 Stuttgart, Germany
Schillersaal

10 Brussels, Belgium
Ancienne Belgique

14 Rotterdam, Holland
Night Town

28 Tel Aviv, Israel
Susan Dalal Auditorium

July 1992

23 Reykjavik, Iceland
Hotel Borg

24 Reykjavik, Iceland
Hotel Borg

30 Louisville, KY USA
Phoenix Hill Tavern

31 Chicago, IL USA
Park West

August 1992

1 Minneapolis, MN USA
1st Avenue

3 Grand Rapids, MI USA
Club Eastbrook

4 Cleveland, OH USA
Peabody's Down Under

5 Cincinnati, OH USA
Bogart's

6 Pittsburgh, PA USA
Rosebud

7 Columbus, OH USA
Newport Music Hall

9 Indianapolis, IN USA
The Vogue

10 Indianapolis, IN USA
City Market

10 Bloomington, IN USA
Jake's

11 Nashville, TN USA
328 Performance Hall

12 Atlanta, GA USA
Center Stage

14 Jacksonville, FL USA
Club Carousel

15 Tampa FL USA
State Theater

16 West Palm Beach, FL USA
Carefree Theater

17 Orlando, FL USA
Beacham Theater

22 Los Angeles, CA USA
Henry Fonda Theater

23 Los Angeles, CA USA
Henry Fonda Theater

24 Los Angeles, CA USA
Henry Fonda Theater

25 Santa Barbara, CA USA
Anaconda Theater

26 San Diego, CA USA
Mandeville Auditorium

28 Portland, OR USA
Roseland Theater

29 Seattle, WA USA
Moore Theater

30 Eugene, OR USA
WOW Hall

September 1992

1 Salt Lake City, UT USA
Murphy Park Amphitheater

2 San Francisco, CA USA
Palace of Fine Arts

3 Sacramento, CA USA
Crest Theater

4 San Juan Capistrano, CA USA
The Coach House

5 San Juan Capistrano, CA USA
The Coach House

11 New Orleans, LA USA
Storyville

12 Mobile, AL USA
The Lumberyard

13 Washington, DC USA
Lisner Auditorium

14 Richmond, VA USA
Flood Zone

16 Fredericksburg, VA USA
Dodd Auditorium

17 Charlottesville, VA USA
Cabell Hall

18 Norfolk, VA USA
Boathouse

19 Raleigh, NC USA
Rialto Theater

20 Charleston, WV USA
Cultural Center Auditorium

22 Knoxville, TN USA
Bijou Theater

24 Athens, GA USA
Fine Arts Auditorium

25 Baton Rouge, LA USA
The Varsity

26 Houston, TX USA
Tower Theater

28 Albuquerque, NM USA
Kimo Theater

29 Boulder, CO USA
Boulder Theater

30 Phoenix, AZ USA
Valley Art Theater

October 1992

1 Phoenix, AZ USA
Valley Art Theater

3 Austin, TX USA
Terrace Ballroom

5 Norman, OK USA
Sooner Theater

6 St. Louis, MO USA
Mississippi Nights

8 New York, NY USA
Town Hall

9 New York, NY USA
Town Hall

11 Red Bank, NJ USA
Count Basie Theater

12 New York, NY USA
Town Hall

18 Boston, MA USA
Berklee Performance Center

20 Glenside, PA USA
Keswick Theater

21 Glenside, PA USA
Keswick Theater

23 Buffalo, NY USA
Rockwell Hall

25 Amherst, MA USA
Buckley Recital Hall

27 Ottawa, Ontario Canada
The Penguin

28 Toronto, Ontario Canada
Phoenix Concert Theatre

29 Montreal, Quebec Canada
Café Campus

30 Detroit, MI USA
St. Andrew's Hall

November 1992

1 New Brunswick, NJ USA
Cook College

2 Cleveland, OH USA
Shooters Live

3 Kalamazoo, MI USA
State Theater

5 Milwaukee, WI USA
Weasler Auditorium

6 Purchase, NY USA
Performing Arts Center

8 Albany, NY USA
Page Hall

9 New Haven, CT USA
Toad's Place

10 Danbury, CT USA
Tuxedo Junction

11 Baltimore, MD USA
Steeltown

12 Baltimore, MD USA
Steeltown

14 DeKalb, IL USA
Boutelle Music Hall

15 Madison, WI USA
Barrymore Theater

21 Perth, Australia
The Octagon

22 Melbourne, Australia
Athenaeum Theatre

23 Melbourne, Australia
Athenaeum Theatre

25 Sydney, Australia
York Theatre

26 Sydney, Australia
York Theatre

27 Sydney, Australia
York Theatre

30 Auckland, New Zealand
Town Hall

Under The Pink Tour 1994

February 1994

24 Newcastle, England
Upon Tyne Theatre

25 Warwick, England
Arts Centre

27 Glasgow, Scotland
Pavilion

28 Edinburgh, Scotland
Queenshall

March 1994

1 Manchester, England
Free Trade Hall

3 Leeds, England
City Varieties Music Hall

4 Cambridge, England
Corn Exchange

6 London, England
Her Majesty's Theatre

7 Bristol, England
Colston Hall

20 Seattle, WA USA
Meany Hall

21 San Francisco, CA USA
Herbst Theater

22 Los Angeles, CA USA
Wadsworth Theater

24 Chicago, IL USA
Vic Theater

26 Toronto, Ontario Canada
Convocation Hall

27 Washington DC USA
Lisner Auditorium

28 Glenside, PA USA
Keswick Theater

30 New York, NY USA
Symphony Space

31 Boston, MA USA
The Sanders Theater

April 1994

1 Atlanta, GA USA
Center Stage

2 Montreal, Quebec Canada
Theatre L'Olympia

5 Paris, France
The Cigalle

6 Brussels, Belgium
Passage 44

7 Amsterdam, Holland
Paradiso

9 Berlin, Germany
Trinitatiskrine

10 Hamburg, Germany
CCH2

12 Frankfurt, Germany
Mozartsaal

13 Dusseldorf, Germany
Schumann Saal

14 Stuttgart, Germany
Kleine Liedehalle

15 Munich, Germany
Prinz Regent

17 Zurich, Switzerland
Tonhalle

18 Milan, Italy
Nacionalle

19 Rome, Italy
Palladium

21 Portsmouth, England
Guildhall

22 Nottingham, England
Royal Centre

23 Ipswich, England
Regent

24 York, England
Barbican

26 Cardiff, Wales
St. David's Hall

28 London, England
Palladium

29 London, England
Palladium

30 London, England
Palladium

May 1994

2 Wolverhampton, England
Civic Hall

3 Belfast, Ireland
Church House

4 Dublin, Ireland
Olympia

5 Stockholm, Sweden
Cirkus

7 Maastricht, Holland
Mecc Conference Center

8 Nijmegen, Holland
Vereeniging

9 Scheveninger, Holland
Irkus Theatre

June 1994

7 Brookville, NY USA
Tilles Center

8 Peekskill, NY USA
Paramount Center For The Arts

10 Rochester, NY USA
Theater On The Ridge

11 Boston, MA
Orpheum Theater

13 New Haven, CT USA
Palace PAC

15 New York, NY USA
Beacon Theater

16 New York, NY USA
Beacon Theater

17 New Brunswick, NJ USA
State Theater

18 Upper Darby, PA USA
Tower Theater

20 Washington, DC USA
Warner Theater

21 Washington, DC USA
Warner Theater

22 Washington, DC USA
Warner Theater

24 Providence, RI USA
The Strand

25 Portland, ME USA
State Theater

26 Burlington, VT USA
Flynn Theater

27 Albany, NY USA
Palace Theater

29 Syracuse, NY USA
Landmark Theater

30 Buffalo, NY USA
Riviera Theater

July 1994

1 Pittsburgh, PA USA
Fulton Theater

2 Detroit, MI USA
State Theater

4 Detroit, MI USA
State Theater

5 Columbus, OH USA
Palace Theater

6 Grand Rapids, MI USA
DeVos Hall

7 Cleveland, OH USA
Cleveland Music Hall

9 Chicago, IL USA
Bismark Theater

11 Madison, WI USA
Barrymore Theater

12 Milwaukee, WI USA
Pabst Theater

13 Cedar Rapids, IA USA
Paramount Theater

14 Minneapolis, MN USA
State Theater

16 Indianapolis, IN USA
Murat Theater

17 Louisville, KY USA
Macauley Theater

18 St. Louis, MO USA
American Theater

19 Kansas City, MO USA
Midland Theater

21 Memphis, TN USA
Orpheum Theater

23 Knoxville, TN USA
Tennessee Theater

24 Richmond, VA USA
Carpenter Center

25 Baltimore, MD USA
Meyerhoff Symphony Hall

27 Norfolk, VA USA
Harrison Opera House

28 Asheville, NC USA
Thomas Wolfe Auditorium

29 Raleigh, NC USA
Raleigh Memorial Auditorium

30 Charlotte, NC USA
Blumenthal Performing Arts

August 1994

1 Kissimmee, FL USA
Tupperware Theater

2 West Palm Beach, FL USA
Kravis Center

3 Tampa, FL USA
Tampa Theater

5 Atlanta, GA USA
Atlanta Symphony Hall

6 Atlanta, GA USA
Atlanta Symphony Hall

8 Nashville, TN USA
Ryman Auditorium

11 New Orleans, LA USA
Orpheum Theater

12 Houston, TX USA
Cullen Performance Hall

13 Austin, TX USA
The Backyard

14 Dallas, TX USA
Majestic Theater

16 Oklahoma City, OK USA
Music Hall

18 Albuquerque, NM USA
Pope Joy Hall

19 Phoenix, AZ USA
Symphony Hall

20 Las Vegas, NV USA
Artemus Hall

21 San Diego, CA USA
Symphony Hall

23 Los Angeles, CA USA
Pantages Theater

24 Los Angeles, CA USA
Pantages Theater

25 Los Angeles, CA USA
Pantages Theater

27 Irvine, CA USA
Crawford Hall

28 Santa Barbara, CA USA
Arlington Theater

30 San Jose, CA USA
Center For The Performing Arts

31 San Francisco, CA USA
Orpheum Theater

September 1994

1 San Francisco, CA USA
Orpheum Theater

8 Santa Rosa, CA USA
Luther Burbank Center

9 Sacramento, CA USA
Sacramento Community Theater

10 Berkeley, CA USA
Zellerbach Auditorium

12 Eugene, OR USA
Hult Center

13 Portland, OR USA
Civic Auditorium

14 Seattle, WA USA
Opera House

15 Bellingham, WA USA
Mt. Baker Theater

17 Salt Lake City, UT USA
Cottonwood High School

19 Denver, CO USA
Paramount Theater

20 Boulder, CO USA
Mackey Auditorium

22 Ames, IA USA
Stephens Auditorium

23 Lawrence, KS USA
Lied Center

24 St. Louis, MO USA
American Theater

26 Dekalb, IL USA
Egyptian Theater

27 Champaign, IL USA
Virginia Theater

28 Carbondale, IL USA
Shryock Auditorium

29 Columbia, MO USA
Missouri Theater

October 1994

1 Evanston, IL USA
Northwestern University

2 Green Bay, WI USA
Weidner Center UW

4 Madison, WI USA
Madison Civic Center

5 Milwaukee, WI USA
Riverside Theater

7 Ann Arbor, MI USA
Ann Arbor Theater

8 Cincinnati, OH USA
Taft Theater

10 South Bend, IN USA
Morris Civic Auditorium

11 Bloomington, IN USA
Indiana University

12 Kalamazoo, MI USA
State Theater

13 Toledo, OH USA
Masonic Auditorium

15 Ann Arbor, MI USA
Hill Auditorium

16 East Lansing, MI USA
Wharton Center

20 Northampton, MA USA
John M. Green Hall

21 Oreno, ME USA
Maine Center For The Arts

22 Storrs, CT USA
Jorgenson Auditorium

23 University Park, PA USA
Eisenhower Auditorium

25 Elmira, NY USA
Clemens Center

26 New Haven, CT USA
Palace Theater

29 Toronto, Ontario Canada
Massey Hall

31 London, Ontario Canada
Centennial Hall

November 1994

1 Kitchener, Ontario Canada
Centre In The Square

2 Windsor, Ontario Canada
Cleary Auditorium

3 Ottawa, Ontario Canada
National Arts Centre

5 Hamilton, Ontario Canada
Hamilton Place

Boys For Pele Tour
1996

6 Kingston, Ontario Canada
Grant Hall

7 Sainte Foy, Quebec Canada
Salle Albert-Rosseau

8 Montreal, Quebec Canada
Sainte Denis Theater

22 Tokyo, Japan
Club Quattro

23 Tokyo, Japan
Nihon Seinenkan Hall

24 Tokyo, Japan
Music Hall

30 Auckland, New Zealand
Town Hall

December 1994

2 Melbourne, Australia
Concert Hall

3 Melbourne, Australia
Concert Hall

4 Brisbane, Australia
Concert Hall

6 Sydney, Australia
State Theatre

7 Sydney, Australia
State Theatre

8 Sydney, Australia
State Theatre

10 Adelaide, Australia
Festival Theatre

12 Perth, Australia
Concert Hall

13 Perth, Australia
Concert Hall

February 1996

23 Ipswich, England
Ipswich Regent

24 Sheffield, England
Sheffield City Hall

25 Manchester, England
Manchester Apollo

27 Edinburgh, Scotland
Edinburgh Usher Hall

28 Aberdeen, Scotland
Aberdeen Capital

29 Glasgow, Scotland
Glasgow Royal Concert Hall

March 1996

1 Hull, England
Hull City Hall

3 Nottingham, England
Nottingham Royal Centre

4 Liverpool, England
Liverpool Philharmonic

5 Newcastle, England
Newcastle City Hall

6 Wolverhampton, England
Wolverhampton Civic Hall

8 London, England
Royal Albert Hall

9 London, England
Royal Albert Hall

11 Exeter, England
Exeter University

12 Bristol, England
Bristol Colston Hall

13 Portsmouth, England
Portsmouth Guild Hall

15 Den Haag, Holland
Congresbouw

16 Amsterdam, Holland
Rai Congrescentrum

18 Paris, France
Grand Rex

19 Dusseldorf, Germany
Philipshalle

20 Hamburg, Germany
CCH1

21 Brussels, Belgium
Royal Circus

22 Stuttgart, Germany
Beethovensaal

24 Frankfurt, Germany
Alte Opera

25 Berlin, Germany
Friedrichstadpalasat

26 Munich, Germany
Philharmonie

27 Vienna, Austria
Austria Centre

29 Milan, Italy
Italiteatro

April 1996

9 Tampa, FL USA
Tampa Bay Performing Arts Center

10 Gainesville, FL USA
Performing Arts Center

11 † New York, NY USA
Majestic Theater

12 Ft. Lauderdale, FL USA
Sunrise Music Theater

13 Orlando, FL USA
University Of Central Florida Arena

14 Atlanta, GA USA
Fox Theater

16 Nashville, TN USA
Tennessee Performing Arts Center

17 Memphis, TN USA
Orpheum Theater

19 Louisville, KY USA
Palace Theater

20 Lexington, KY USA
Singletary Center For The Arts

21 Asheville, NC USA
Thomas Wolfe Auditorium

23 Knoxville, TN USA
Civic Auditorium

24 Columbia, SC USA
The Township

26 Washington, DC USA
Constitution Hall

27 Washington, DC USA
Constitution Hall

28 Washington, DC USA
Constitution Hall

May 1996

1 Philadelphia, PA USA
Tower Theater

2 Philadelphia, PA USA
Tower Theater

3 Philadelphia, PA USA
Tower Theater

5 Montreal, Quebec Canada
St. Denis

6 Montreal, Quebec Canada
St. Denis

7 Burlington, VT USA
Auditorium

8 Durham, NH USA
UNH Arena

10 Albany, NY USA
Palace Theater

11 New Haven, CT USA
Palace Theater

13 New York, NY USA
Virgin Megastore In-
Store...*appearance broadcast
simultaneously on the Internet*

13 New York, NY USA
The Paramount

14 New York, NY USA
The Paramount

15 New York, NY USA
The Paramount

17 Springfield, MA USA
Symphony Hall

18 Syracuse, NY
Landmark Theater

19 Wilkes-Barre, PA USA
Kirby Center

21 Boston, MA USA
Wang Center

22 Boston, MA USA
Wang Center

25 Buffalo, NY USA
Shea's Performing Arts Center

26 London, Ontario Canada
Alumni Hall

27 Toronto, Ontario Canada
Massey Hall

28 Toronto, Ontario Canada
Massey Hall

30 Pittsburgh, PA USA
Benedum Center

31 Detroit, MI USA
Fox Theater

June 1996

2 Grand Rapids, MI USA
Welsh Auditorium

3 Cincinnati, OH USA
Aranoff Center

4 Cleveland, OH USA
Music Hall

6 Chicago, IL USA
Rosemont Theater

7 Chicago, IL USA
Rosemont Theater

8 Milwaukee, WI USA
Riverside Theater

10 Minneapolis, MN USA
Northrup Auditorium

11 Ames, IA USA
Stephens Auditorium

12 St. Louis, MO USA
Fox Theater

13 Kansas City, KS USA
Memorial Hall

15 Dallas, TX USA
Bronco Bowl

16 Austin, TX USA
The Backyard

17 Houston, TX USA
Cullen Auditorium

19 Denver, CO USA
Paramount Theater

20 Denver, CO USA
Paramount Theater

21 Salt Lake City, UT USA
Abravanel Hall

23 Santa Barbara, CA USA
County Bowl

24 Las Vegas, NV USA
Aladdin Theater

26 San Diego, CA USA
Civic Theater

27 San Diego, CA USA
Civic Theater

28 Los Angeles, CA USA
The Greek

29 Los Angeles, CA USA
The Greek

30 Los Angeles, CA USA
The Greek

July 1996

2 Phoenix, AZ USA
Symphony Hall

10 Sacramento, CA USA
Community Theater

11 Oakland, CA USA
Paramount Theater

12 Oakland, CA USA
Paramount Theater

14 San Jose, CA USA
San Jose State Events Center

16 Seattle, WA USA
Paramount Theater

17 Seattle, WA USA
Paramount Theater

19 Vancouver, BC Canada
Orpheum Theatre

20 Eugene, OR USA
Hult Center

21 Portland, OR USA
Schnitzer Auditorium

23 Boise, ID USA
Morrison PAC

26 Cedar Rapids, IA USA
Paramount

27 Springfield, IL USA
Sagamon State University

28 Indianapolis, IN USA
Murat Theater

29 Peoria, IL USA
Peoria Civic Center

31 Toledo, OH USA
Stranahan

August 1996

1 Columbus, OH USA
Palace Theater

3 Dayton, OH USA
Memorial Auditorium

4 Chattanooga, TN USA
Tivoli Theater

5 Birmingham, AL USA
Alabama Theater

7 Jackson, MS USA
Thaila Mara Hall

8 Atlanta, GA USA
Chastain Park Ampitheater

10 Pensacola, FL USA
Bayfront Auditorium

11 Jacksonville, FL USA
Florida Theater

15 Raleigh, NC USA
Raleigh Memorial Auditorium

16 Vienna, VA USA
Wolf Trap

17 Richmond, VA USA
Carpenter Center

19 Norfolk, VA USA
Chrysler Hall

21 Charlotte, NC USA
Owens Auditorium

22 Greensboro, NC USA
War Memorial Auditorium

24 Providence, RI USA
Providence PAC

25 Wantaugh, NY USA
Jones Beach Theater

26 Holmdel, NJ USA
Garden State Arts Center

28 Buffalo, NY USA
Artpark

29 Rochester, NY USA
Finger Lakes PAC

September 1996

1 Wallingford, CT USA
Oakdale Theater

9 Boston, MA USA
Harborlights Pavillion

10 Poughkeepsie, NY USA
Mid-Hudson Civic Center

12 Erie, PA USA
Warner Theater

13 University Park, PA USA
Eisenhower Auditorium

14 Pittsburgh, PA USA
Palumbo Theater

16 Akron, OH USA
EJ Thomas PAC

18 Muncie, IN USA
Emens Auditorium

19 Bloomington, IN USA
Indiana University Auditorium

20 Rockford, IL USA
Coronado Theater

22 Green Bay, WI USA
Weidner Center

23 Madison, WI USA
Oscar Meyer Theater

24 Normal, IL USA
Braden Auditorium

26 East Lansing, MI USA
Wharton Center

27 Ann Arbor, MI USA
Hill Auditorium

28 Chicago, IL USA
Arie Crown Theater

30 Baltimore, MD USA
Lyric Theater

October 1996

1 Baltimore, MD USA
Lyric Theater

2 New Brunswick, NJ USA
State Theater

5 Williamsport, PA USA
Community Arts Center

6 Binghamton, NY USA
Anderson PAC

7 Buffalo, NY USA
Center For The Arts Mainstage

9 Charleston, SC USA
Galliard Municipal Auditorium

10 Athens, GA USA
Classic Center Theater

11 Roanoke, VA USA
Roanoke Civic Auditorium

13 Little Rock, AR USA
Robinson Center

14 Lafayette, LA USA
Heyman PAC

16 New Orleans, LA USA
Saenger Theater

18 Melbourne, FL USA
Maxwell King Center

19 Clearwater, FL USA
Ruth Eckerd Hall

20 Ft. Myers, FL USA
Barbara Mann Auditorium

22 Miami, FL USA
Jackie Gleason Theater

23 Miami, FL USA
Jackie Gleason Theater

24 West Palm Beach, FL USA
Kravis Center

25 West Palm Beach, FL USA
Kravis Center

27 San Antonio, TX USA
Majestic Theater

28 College Station, TX USA
Rudder Auditorium

29 Lubbock, TX USA
Municipal Auditorium

30 Oklahoma City, OK USA
Civic Center Music Hall

November 1996

2 Tulsa, OK USA
Brady Theater

3 Lawrence, KS USA
Lied Center

4 Springfield, MO USA
Hammons PAC

6 Davenport, IA USA
Adler Theater

7 Omaha, NE USA
Orpheum Theater

9 Albuquerque, NM USA
Pope Joy Hall

10 Boulder, CO USA
Macky Auditorium

11 Boulder, CO USA
Macky Auditorium

December 1996

13 Los Angeles, CA USA
Universal Ampitheater
"KROQ Almost Acoustic Christmas
Concert" for Charity (tickets sold
out in 13 minutes)

1997

January 1997

23 New York, NY USA
The Theater at Madison Square
Garden (Benefit Concert for
RAINN)

MTV Unplugged: Postcard

† Thursday, April 11th 1996...*Tori flew to New York City from Florida after playing only two dates in the US and recorded an episode of MTV Unplugged. The Show was recorded at the Brooklyn Academy Of Music's Majestic Theater and was first broadcast in the US on June 25th 1996. The following is the original set list as it was written by Tori*:

Leather / Mr. Zebra / Blood Roses / Putting The Damage On / Cornflake Girl / Doughnut Song / In The Springtime Of His Voodoo / Silent All These Years / Precious Things / Marianne / Caught A Lite Sneeze / Me and A Gun

(*Encore*) Over The Rainbow / Hey Jupiter

The actual set Tori played was somewhat different:

Leather / Blood Roses (*with harpsichord*) / Putting The Damage On / Cornflake Girl (*three takes*) Doughnut Song / In The Springtime Of His Voodoo / Silent All These Years

At this point in the show, during Silent All These Years, *Tori left the stage declaring "I'm going to find the girl who plays the piano."*

Upon returning after a short time:

Marianne / Silent All These Years (*all the way through this time*) / Precious Things / Icicle / Caught A Lite Sneeze (*with harpsichord and piano*) / Me And A Gun

(*Encore*) Over The Rainbow / Hey Jupiter / Honey / Space Dog / In The Springtime Of His Voodoo

The actual MTV broadcast on June 25th, 1996 consisted of only eight tracks:

1 Cornflake Girl
2 Blood Roses (*harpsichord*)
3 Silent All These Years
4 Icicle
5 Caught A Lite Sneeze (*harpsichord and piano*)
6 Over The Rainbow
7 Hey Jupiter
8 In The Springtime Of His Voodoo

10

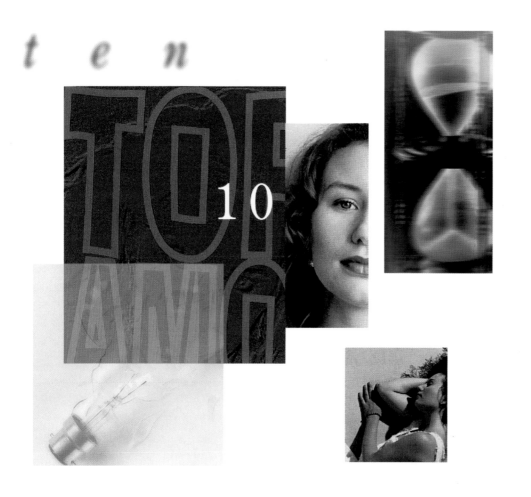

chapter ten
timeline

1963.......22 August, Myra Ellen Amos born in Newton, NC USA

1965.......Begins playing piano at age 2

1968.......Enters Baltimore's Peabody Conservatory as 5-year-old prodigy, the youngest student ever accepted at the prestigious Peabody

1973.......Expelled from Peabody Conservatory for insisting on playing by ear instead of learning to read music correctly

1973.......Attends first rock concert: Elton John

1974.......Writes first song (*More Than Just A Friend*) at age 12

1975.......Fails audition to re-enter Peabody Conservatory

1977.......Wins "County Teen Talent Contest"

1977.......Begins playing live in clubs and gay bars in and around Washington, DC and Baltimore, MD USA

1980.......Records Baltimore 7" single at age 17, co-written with brother Mike

1981.......Plays two-month gig at The Hilton Hotel, Myrtle Beach, SC USA

1982/83 ..Plays The Sheraton-Carlton Hotel in Washington, DC USA off and on throughout 1982-1983

1983.......Ellen Amos changes name to Tori after a friend's boyfriend convinced her she looked more like a "Tori" than an "Ellen"

1983.......Records demo for Narada Michael Walden in San Francisco

1984.......September, moves to Los Angeles, begins playing bars and lounges

1984.......Beats out Sarah Jessica Parker for role in Kellogg's "Just Right" TV commercial

1985.......Decides to give up the piano, forms *Y Kant Tori Read*

1987.......Signs to Atlantic Records, begins work on *Y Kant Tori Read* album

1988.......June, *Big Picture* 7" single released in the US

1988.......July, *Y Kant Tori Read* album released in the US

1988.......August, *Cool On Your Island* 7" single released in the US

1988.......Fall, Begins to play the piano again after the failure of the *Y Kant Tori Read* persona

1989.......Atlantic gives Tori six months to come up with a new album

1989.......Begins work on what would become *Little Earthquakes*

1990.......December, Atlantic rejects new album

1991.......January, continues to write new material

1991.......February, Moves to London at the behest of Atlantic Records' Doug Morris, begins playing small clubs and bars.

1991.......Spring, Meets and begins working relationship with Cindy Palmano

1991.......October, *Me And A Gun* single released in the UK and Germany

1991.......November, *Silent All These Years* picked as "Single Of The Week" at BBC Radio One, London

1991.......November, *Silent All These Years* (reissue of *Me And A Gun*) single released in the UK

1992.......January, *China* single released in the UK

1992.......January, *Little Earthquakes* released in the UK

1992.......January, *Little Earthquakes* tour begins in England

1992.......February, *Little Earthquakes* released in the US

1992.......March, *Winter* singles released in the UK

1992.......April, *Little Earthquakes* released in Japan

1992.......April, *Silent All These Years* single released in Japan

1992.......May, *Crucify* single released in the US

1992.......June, *Crucify* singles released in the UK

1992.......August, *Silent All These Years* singles re-issued in the UK

1992.......November, *Toys* soundtrack released featuring Tori's *The Happy Worker*

1992.......November, *Winter* single released in the US

1992.......November, Little Earthquakes tour finishes in New Zealand

1994.......January, *Cornflake Girl* singles released in the UK

1994.......January, *Under The Pink* released in the UK

1994.......February, *God* single released in the US, number one Billboard M/R Chart

1994.......February, *Under The Pink* released in the US and Japan

1994.......February, Under The Pink tour begins in England

1994.......March, *Pretty Good Year* singles released in the UK

1994.......April, *Cornflake Girl* single released in the US

1994.......May, *Past The Mission* singles released in the UK

1994.......August, *God* single released in the UK

1994.......December, Under The Pink tour finishes in Australia

1995.......January, *Higher Learning* soundtrack released featuring a new song, *Butterfly* and also Tori covering REM's *Losing My Religion*

1995.......April, Tori duets with Robert Plant on *Down By The Seaside*

1995.......October, Tori duets with Tom Jones on *I Wanna Get Back With You*

1995.......November, *You Sleigh Me*, including *Little Drummer Boy* released

1996.......January, *Caught A Lite Sneeze* singles released in the UK and US

1996.......January, *Boys For Pele* released in the UK and US

1996.......February, *Boys For Pele* tour begins in England

1996.......February, *Boys For Pele* released in Japan with bonus track *Mr. Toodles*

1996.......March, *Talula* singles released in the UK

1996.......May, Tori broadcasts live in-store appearance on the Internet from the Virgin Megastore in New York

1996.......May, *Talula* single released in the US

1996.......May, *Twister* soundtrack released including *Talula* (*BT's Tornado Mix*)

1996.......June, Atlantic ships *Professional Widow* promo 12" to clubs

1996.......June, MTV broadcasts "Tori Unplugged" recorded in April, 1996

1996.......July, *Professional Widow* single released in the US

1996.......July, *Professional Widow* hits number one on Billboard's Club Play Chart

1996.......July, *Hey Jupiter* single released in the UK

1996.......August, *Hey Jupiter* EP released in the US

1996.......September, Atlantic ships *In The Springtime Of His Voodoo* promo 12" single to clubs

1996.......September, *In The Springtime Of His Voodoo* single released in US

1996.......October, VH1 *Crossroads* CD released in US featuring *I'm On Fire*

1996.......November, *Boys For Pele* tour finishes

1997.......January, performs benefit concert for RAINN at The Theater at Madison Square Garden, New York, NY

appendix

glossary

Acetate

Acetates are actually aluminum discs coated in a soft vinyl-like material called lacquer. They are intended to be played only a few times because the soft material wears out very quickly. Acetates are frequently 1-sided and are highly sought after as only a extremely small number are ever made for the artist and producer to use as a reference. Acetates often contain unreleased versions or remixes of tracks that do not appear on the finished record. The acetate of *Silent All These Years* is remixed to fade out gradually.

CD-R

CD-Rs or Reference CDs are now usually used in place of acetates or test pressings. These allow the artist and producer to hear the work before it is delivered to the label as finished or to provide a quick advance copy of the finished work. CD-Rs can only be recorded one time. CD-Rs are usually packaged in a plain jewel case with an insert from the studio containing information regarding the recording. Because of their relatively small numbers, CD-Rs are extremely collectible and valuable.

Test Pressing

A "Test Pressing" is a record made in very small numbers to check sound quality before a record is finally manufactured in quantity. Test pressings usually have white labels and a white sleeve with all the album's pertinent information either on the sleeve or on the labels. Because of their extremely limited numbers, test pressings are considered to be among the rarest items of virtually any artist.

Promotional Record

A promotional copy of a recording is actually a commercial, or stock copy, that will be distributed—usually prior to the album's release—to retail stores, the press and radio. A promotional copy has been marked either by a gold stamp, a sticker or a cut or hole to indicate that it is promotional and cannot be sold to the public or returned to the record company for credit. Promotional copies are very common and in some cases less valuable than commercial copies; as in the case of the *Y Kant Tori Read* LP.

Promotional-Only Record

Promotional-only records are never intended for commercial release and as such are pressed in relatively small quantities. They are distributed to radio, retail stores, DJs, the press and sometimes given away to the public as part of the promotion of a new record. E.g.: the *London Girls* French CD single. Promotional-only copies are usually a single intended for radio, e.g.: *I'm On Fire*, a collection of tracks that does not appear commercially, e.g.: *New Music From Tori Amos*...or an interview, e.g.: *Tea With The Waitress*. The easiest way to distinguish promotional-only copies from commercial copies is by their lack of a UPC number or bar code. Promotional-only copies frequently contain rare material, such as live tracks, remixes or previously unreleased songs. Because of their limited numbers, promotional-only copies are rare and highly sought after by collectors.